Longings, Laughter & Laments

Writers of the Forest

Thank you to our families and friends for supporting us through a time of unprecedented unrest throughout our country as well as a global pandemic that impacted all. Without your listening, reading, and critiquing, we would not have produced this anthology. We wrote from our hearts about our longings and laments, often with laughter when we observed the lighter side of life. We are grateful for your continued encouragement.

--Writers of the Forest

Longings, Laughter & Laments
Copyright © 2021 by the Writers of the Forest

All rights reserved. Any use, storage, reproduction or transmission in any form or by any means of the contents without the written consent of the author is prohibited.

Contributing Authors: Claudia Blanchard, Terry L. Dismore, Barbara Dullaghan, Lorraine Gilmore, Lee Norman Mehler, Diane Pascoe, John Stickney, John C. Stipa, Suzy Tenenbaum

Editors: Claudia Blanchard, John Stipa

Cover art: Lee Norman Mehler

Sales of this book without a front cover are unauthorized.

Disclaimer: Each story contained in this book is based on the contributing author's imagination or recollections of events, related to the best of his or her knowledge. No errors, oversights or harm were intended for any individual, organization or company.

Amazon Digital Services LLC
410 Terry Avenue North
Seattle, WA 98109
October 25, 2021

ISBN-13: 979-8-474-10246-7

Library of Congress Control Number: 2021919914

WHO ARE THE WRITERS OF THE FOREST?

Every week we gather, people who share a love of writing and who value one another's friendship and insight. We document the life that surrounds us, or start from prompts that spark a new piece of fiction, non-fiction, or poetry.

The prompts are open to interpretation to stimulate our creativity. Think for yourself where your imagination runs after you hear: "They never saw it coming."

We thoughtfully review the work of our fellow writers, urging them to continue, or to improve what they have started.

Our ultimate goal is to apply our artistic skills and literary efforts to take the reader to another place, another time, or even another world.

Table of Contents

Life Lessons From The Letter "L"	Suzy Tenenbaum	3
Super Pink Moon	John Stickney	5
Moon Pen to Paper	John Stickney	6
Dusk	John Stickney	7
Green Giant	Claudia Blanchard	8
Free to be Me	Terry L. Dismore	10
The First	Lee Norman Mehler	11
Nursery Rhyme Mash Up	Lorraine Gilmore	14
Can You Guess What This Is?	Suzy Tenenbaum	16
Treasures	Barbara Dullaghan	18
Plankton	John Stickney	19
Lost Car	Claudia Blanchard	20
My Child Didn't Come Home Last Night	Terry L. Dismore	21
The Zipline	Lee Norman Mehler	22
Romancing The Drink	Lorraine Gilmore	26
Leaning In and Leaning on	Suzy Tenenbaum	31
The House I Used to Live In	John Stickney	32
It Can Be Done	John C. Stipa	33
BOOM!	Lee Norman Mehler	35
Again	Diane Pascoe	38
Backyard Tweets	Suzy Tenenbaum	40
There is a Storm Coming	Terry L. Dismore	42
At The Museum	Claudia Blanchard	44
Old Friends	Lorraine Gilmore	45
Sorry	John Stickney	48
Leaving	Lee Norman Mehler	51
Endurance	Barbara Dullaghan	54
A Vessel Not A Vase	Terry L. Dismore	55
Don't Give Up	Diane Pascoe	57
Blue Beautiful Blue	Suzy Tenenbaum	60
Thou Shall Not Kill	Claudia Blanchard	62
The Train	Lee Norman Mehler	63
Summer's Edge	John Stickney	66
Waiting For The Wife	Lorraine Gilmore	67
Woke Up This Morning	Terry L. Dismore	70
That Damned Owl	Barbara Dullaghan	71
The Collar	Diane Pascoe	73
An Unexpected Kindness	Diane Pascoe	75
Time Lock	John Stickney	78

Celebrate Earth Day	Claudia Blanchard	81
My Super Power	Lorraine Gilmore	82
Quiet	Terry L. Dismore	85
SADness My Old Friend	John C. Stipa	87
Lucky Duck	Suzy Tenenbaum	89
The Recipe	Lee Norman Mehler	90
Cold Sweat	John Stickney	96
Still Feel All of That Love From Here	Lorraine Gilmore	98
Love is Love	Terry L. Dismore	101
Limerick in Blue 1	Claudia Blanchard	102
Limerick in Blue 2	Claudia Blanchard	103
Plugging Into the Future	Diane Pascoe	104
Aunt Edith	Lorraine Gilmore	107
Isn't Life Just Like That?	Suzy Tenenbaum	110
Animals and Tools, Tools and Animals	John Stickney	113
The Repo Man Sucks Wind	Lee Norman Mehler	115
It Started to Rain	Terry L. Dismore	118
Josie	Barbara Dullaghan	119
Deleted	John Stickney	121
Cupboard Conversations	Suzy Tenenbaum	124
The Real Story of Cinderella	Lorraine Gilmore	125
Sunrise Sunset	Terry L. Dismore	128
'Twas Beauty Killed the Beast	Claudia Blanchard	129
What We Threw At The Monster	John Stickney	130
Fragile	Suzy Tenenbaum	132
Finality	Lorraine Gilmore	133
In Honor of Women's History Month	Terry L. Dismore	135
When Day and Night is a Short Story	John Stickney	138
The Keys of Life	Lee Norman Mehler	139

Novel Excerpts:

The Relentless Anchor	John C. Stipa	150
Guilt Will Lead the Way	Barbara Dullaghan	153
When Ink Bleeds	John C. Stipa	163

Author Biographies	167

"You only live once, but if you do it right, once is enough."
- *Mae West*

Life Lessons from the Letter L

By: Suzy Tenenbaum

Limit your laments
    The past is gone

Languish in your longings
    Only if they motivate you

Laugh often and be playful
    Let the child in you remain alive

Lean on loved ones
    When times are tough

Liberate yourself from
    Others' expectations

Learn, learn, learn
    Never stop

Listen to the stories of people not like you
    We are so different and so alike

Lend a hand when you can
    Help and accept help

Link arms and be strong
    In your pursuit of justice for all

Lose that inner critic voice
    Tell it you aren't listening to it anymore

Lift up young children and show them the moon
    And other natural wonders of the world

Linger in moments of peace
    And breathe in the calm

Look at life's ups and downs
    As the seesaw of life

Love with open arms,
    An open mind and an open heart

Super Pink Moon (April 26, 2021)

By: John Stickney

This month's moon –
has pink-eye
the small dipper
drips
drops
drips
some medicine
don't rub your
Mr. Moon eyes
and spread it
to the stars
or beyond

Moon Pen to Paper

By: John Stickney

This month's moon
is the inspector
of stars
watching wide eyed
unblinking
noting flaws and motion
taking notes for
next month's moon
next full moon
go outside
listen for the scratch
scratch scratch of
the moon pen
to moon paper
be quiet
let the moon concentrate
on this important work

Dusk

By: John Stickney

A brilliant actor
Ready for the
Moon's spotlight

Green Giant

By: Claudia Blanchard

"Michael! Mary screeched. For the love of god what is going on in our pantry?" Mary jabbed her finger at cans labeled in magic marker with women's names written on them. Christina on the Del Monte quartered artichoke hearts, Terry on the Progresso chicken and corn chowder soup and Lauri scrawled across the can of Green Giant green beans. "And why is it in duplicate? Christina, Christina, Terry, Terry, Lauri, Lauri, two identical cans per person."

"Oh that," Michael chuckled.

"Yeah, that," Mary replied, frowning. Having worked another extra-long shift at the hospital, Mary was in no mood to decipher the parade of women's names marching two by two across her pantry shelf like some Noah's Ark reenactment.

"Calm down Mary. Let me explain. You know the gym is closed and now I meet with my clients using Face Time. I've created a way to improve each of their virtual training sessions by using everyday household items to add weight to their exercises." Michael clearly had a lot of time on his hands now that he is not training his clients at the local gym. And his client load has been greatly reduced (along with his income) because of the quarantine. That, and the fact that his clientele is older and generally not too tech-savvy and this virtual alternative does not appeal to everyone.

"I've been thinking about how to attach ten-pound sacks of potatoes or oranges to each end of a broom so we can bench press and get those pectoral muscles engaged. Mary, any ideas you want to share? I'd be grateful. We're pretty burned out ourselves doing puzzles, playing poker and watching Netflix right? This is a great creativity exercise for us."

Mary shakes her head. "Michael, I'm going to take a hot bath. I need a long, relaxing soak and there had better not be any of your clients' props in the tub."

"Michael!!!"

Free To Be Me

By: Terry L. Dismore

Is it the **melanin** in my skin
spiral tightly coiled hair
my **brown eyes or**
the way I speak with an **accent**?

Are your blue eyes
making a difference
for me to be free?

Blood-stained streets
when all I'm
doing is being **me**

If I can't be **me**
I'm not **free**
people been trying
over 2,000 years
so you tell me how do I
become **free** to be **me**?

Inhale, exhale
same air we all breathe
so why is it different for me
in my quest to be **free and me?**

Contributions to world peace
must include my existence and
freedom to be me

The First

By: Lee Norman Mehler

Arthur looks around the Starlight Ballroom, not sure why he had come, other than Lennie had dragged him here. "Come on," he whispers to himself. "It's Saturday night. You will never have a life if you don't get out there and take a chance."

He wasn't even sure how he and Lennie had become friends. Arthur was a reader, not a doer, whereas Lennie was funny and loved talking to anyone. Arthur liked huddling in the overstuffed chair with the afghan in his living room, a glass of cheap white wine and his feet up. He'd usually turn on the floor console Zenith radio to listen to his favorite big bands or classical piano music after the sun went down.

But some nights Arthur liked the quiet. He wanted to hear the wind blowing outside three stories up. He listened to the stiletto rain pelting the large tenement windows or the steam flowing off the radiator in each room. On warm spring nights, with a glow of the city rising above the rooftops, he would crawl out on the fire escape to smell the cherry blossoms that lined the street below. He was the definition of a loner. But not by choice. Really out of habit.

Deep down Arthur yearned to be different. This is why he let Lennie through the protective wall he had erected around himself. Lennie was the popular guy at work. The one who wasn't afraid of the pretty girls. They often ventured down to Madison Square Garden for a Knickerbocker basketball game in the middle of the week when tickets were cheaper. Lennie talked to any stranger hanging from the overhead straps on the subway. If they were cute and had long legs, the talks lasted until their stop.

Arthur scanned the ballroom looking for a safe corner

to watch life dance by, instead of taking the first step. Lennie prances across the dance floor with a pretty brunette doing the fox trot. The suspended mirror ball bounces hundreds of sparks of lights off the recently painted walls and ceiling of the renovated dance hall. Arthur feels slightly dizzy from the motion of the lights and the dancers. He wanders over to the white linen covered table with the cheese and crackers, and the red punch bowl. He had learned if he held a drink or a plate, he could avoid looking into people's eyes. And he thought if he took a sip every few minutes, he didn't seem so pitiful.

He tips the pewter ladle up over the paper cup.

"Can I offer you a piece of carrot cake?"

The voice light and airy, is rich and soulful. Arthur's eyes move up the soft lines of her slight frame to the blond hair that stops just short of her shoulders. Her smile easy, not exaggerated, puts him at ease. Her face is freckled and perfect. Her eyes, hazel and sparkling with an inner light, draws him in so he can see her truth.

Words back up in his throat. Not unusual for him. But he feels compelled to not hold back. He tries not to stammer.

"I, um…I'm not a fan of carrot. What's that one?" he said, pointing to the cake with powdered sugar dusting the top.

"That's a pistachio and chocolate Bundt marble cake. I made it myself."

"Probably better since you made it," Arthur responds. For once he does not look down.

"I haven't seen you here before," she says.

"No, my buddy Lennie wanted to try this place out. He's the dancer. I'm not much of one."

Her smile doesn't waiver. "Me, too. Kathy likes to come, so we do this sometimes. She's the one in the flower print over there. I like to bake."

"I like to eat," Arthur says, immediately regretting his

attempt to be clever and lighthearted.

She doesn't seem to mind as she quietly laughs. This is new territory he has never crossed before. He read about this in the classic novels he raced through in his thirst for another life.

"There is someone out there for everyone," his grandmother used to say. "You just have to wait for your turn."

This was his turn. She was the first. He knew it.

"I'm Amy.

"I'm Arthur."

Dedicated to my wife who inspires me every day, on the occasion of our 48th wedding anniversary.

Nursery Rhyme Mashup

By: Lorraine Gilmore

We didn't live in a shoe, but my husband and I had many children. Bedtime became more and more of a challenge as time went by. It was bedlam and chaos filled with tears (theirs) and screaming (mine) until the night that I got creative with their bedtime story. For some reason they loved what I made up and it would calm them. As they lay still in their beds, their little eyelids would begin to droop and sleep would overtake them.

Maybe you can stay awake while I read it to you.

Once upon a time in a land far, far away there was a woman who lived in a tiny house filled with children. Some say that she was old, but I know for a fact that this is not so. They thought she was old because she was always tired. That's easy to understand when you think about the dirty clothes that had to be washed, the meals that had to be cooked and served and the shoelaces that needed tying. She never had time to sit and read a book or have a cup of tea.

Early one morning as she began making breakfast for her brood, she saw that the water bucket was empty. She quickly called in the oldest twins and told them to go up the hill to fetch a pail of water, but Jack fell down and broke his crown and Jill came tumbling after. Right away, Wynken, Blyken and Nod, who were triplets, offered to take care of the situation. Wynken and Nod helped Jack to limp home while Blyken brought back the pail of water.

When breakfast was ready, all of them were lifting their spoons to eat their porridge when they saw a strange sight out of the window. Their cow was jumping over the moon. They dashed to the window to watch and with their backs turned to the table, their dishes ran away with their spoons. Their little dog laughed at this strange sight, but the hungry children did not find it one bit funny.

Just then their mom brought out the pie from the oven. It was filled with four and twenty blackbirds and it was their favorite. When she carefully cut into it with a knife, the birds began to sing. The children were not amused. The pie was returned to the oven and they were sent out to play without any breakfast.

The first thing that they saw was their neighbor, Little Bo Peep, crying because she had lost her sheep and didn't know where to find them. Contrary Mary, who was the oldest girl, told her to leave them alone and they would come home. This cheered up Little Bo Peep who then suggested that they could play ring around the rosie. This was going well until they all fell down. Little Georgie Porgie fell so hard that he hurt his bum and began to cry.

After he quit crying …

Oh, are you still awake? At this point in the story all of my children are sound asleep and I have never had to finish it.

This idea came to me at 4:20 this morning. It was inspired by Suzy's challenge.

Can You Guess What This Is?

By: Suzy Tenenbaum

I have a love/hate relationship with this thing in my life

It gets longer
Then it gets shorter

Sometimes it refers to happy things
Sometimes mundane or not so happy

Children don't have this thing
Neither do the elderly

I've complained about this thing
Yet it helps me

This thing is proof that you have a full life
And it can gnaw at you

Here's a hint
Sometimes there are lines drawn through it
Sometimes it has a column of check marks

It's THE LIST
    Birthday card to Betty Lou
    Make dentist appointment
    Buy sneakers
    Call re mom's health insurance
    Schedule rug cleaner

Upon reflection, I'm giving up my resentment of THE LIST

People in war torn countries don't have the luxury of a list

Lucky me to have things to do and places to go
Means for health care and friends to honor

I'm reframing how I think about things
The List is a sign of a full and engaging life

I'll resent it no more

Treasures

By: Barbara Dullaghan

I stand on the beach
If I close my eyes, I can see them
Running, chasing, laughing and squealing with delight

Even when I am alone, they are with me
The inner crab reminding me of youthful wisdom
A barely opened pen shell with help from a smaller Scotch Bonnet
Reminds me that even the smaller ones want to be in the middle

A shark's eye, imperfect from bruises and little scratches
The spiral whelk, knobbed like their knees, smooth but spiny
Held up to their ears to hear the ocean
Sea glass, smooth and perfectly shaded
Above all, a heart-shaped stone says it all
Cousins.

For my grandchildren with love:
Mia, Gemma, Penelope,
Finn, Mila, and Willa

Plankton

By: John Stickney

In this older life
I am taking a supplement*
Derived from the wisest
Of all creatures -
The jellyfish,
To improve my mental
acuity.

Does it work?
My wife asked.

But I could barely hear
her,
Already several fathoms deep
Off the coral coast.

(Based on the actual advertised product *Prevagen)

Lost Car

By: Claudia Blanchard

Lost my car
Spotted a bar
Needed to think
Ordered a drink

My Child Didn't Come Home Last Night

By: Terry L. Dismore

Nothing but a stream of angry tears is all I got today
wipe them away, they just come back
internal hurting won't stop

Good morning Lord
If you hear my cries,
please open your skies
anoint me with your rain
to match my sorrow
and pain

Stop telling me
to switch off the engine
remove the key from the ignition as if
that will replace the fact that
My child didn't come home last night!

Mothers reaching out wanting
me to take a stand
all I want is my child to come home at night
I've been searching all night, but

My child didn't come home last night

The Zipline

By: Lee Norman Mehler

I am always the one holding the towel. I live vicariously, which is fine with me. While others do battle with windmills, I stand on the sideline with their extra lance just in case. I am Sancho Panza in a world full of Don Quixotes. I am less bruised. My body has lasted through more wars, but I wear no medals. I have tasted the victory of others on the edge of their greatness.

The sun blazes down on my broad brimmed hat. My granddaughter, Penelope, is thirty-five feet above on a heavy beamed tower. I hold the beach towel and camera, my head tilted up to not miss a minute.

Words of encouragement above from Trevor, the head counselor. "You can do this, Penelope! It will be fun! Just like flying."

I see my son, Morgan, with his summer beard looking uncertain and knowing that he has to lead by example.

A bit of father-son telepathy enters my brain.

What have I gotten myself into, Dad? my son says without speaking.

Morgan utters uncertain encouragement. "Okay P, you're a good swimmer and this is all over water. Just step off with me."

"I don't know, Daddy. It's so high!"

I wish I could be up on the zipline tower in my granddaughter's place. Oh no, wait! I am Sancho Panza. I guess I wouldn't trade places.

Forty-eight hours earlier, stripped down to our tee shirts and shorts, we had loaded up my son's pickup with sunscreen, bug spray and all the electric fans we could find for our trip. Morgan surprised us taking the long way through Beaufort.

As the salt air splashed us from the front of the ferry, Penelope expressed her excitement. "I want to go motorboating, and kayaking, do archery and tennis!"

"What do you want to do the most?" I asked.

"I want to roast s'mores just like Daddy!"

My heart melted like the coming fate of the marshmallows and chocolate bars.

This was Family Camp near New Bern, NC. I had conceded to accompany my son and granddaughter to Camp Seagull. Morgan had been a camper and boating counselor here twenty-five years before. The price had more than doubled and so had my age. I would participate as much as my old bones would allow.

My son had forgotten one prerequisite for Penelope earning her swimming band – her goggles. My granddaughter panicked when she first hit the murky lake water for her swim test. She got half-way through the treading water and one lap ordeal, when she could go no further. We watched her break down in tears from our distant vantage point outside the fence. When she returned, we did our best to distract and reassure her that she had done her best.

"I am going to try again tomorrow," she said instantly.

I handed her the dry towel, that she had not thrown in, and hoped for the best. Tomorrow, and the day after arrived and that determined little person took and retook the test. Finally, she finished her lap to success, jumped in the air and beamed all the way back to the chain link fence with her purple neck band of victory. By overcoming this, she could sample the other challenges of camp.

Now on the last day, I stand below looking up, holding the same towel. I am once again Sancho Panza while my granddaughter conquers this three-story dragon. I set the camera on sports mode to get every possible frame of greatness. They travel up and up and up trying not to get splinters from the weathered handrails. Finally, they are at the top.

"I'm not sure, Daddy."

Trevor, the expert at pushing small children over the edge of the precipice into the chasm of uncertainty, suggests, "Try sitting on your butt, your back to the lake, Penelope."

She hesitates, but sits down and inches to the edge. They check the safety line above and all the harness connections.

Morgan says, "Okay, let's do this on three!" He counts, "One…two…three" and he pushes off… by himself. But surprisingly Penelope is one count behind as she kicks away from the tiny platform. She screams with glee as she soars into the bright afternoon sun.

The birds settle down after the small human interloper passes through their territory. I realize being Sancho Panza to my granddaughter's knight in shining armor is an honor I won't soon forget, especially if the photos come out.

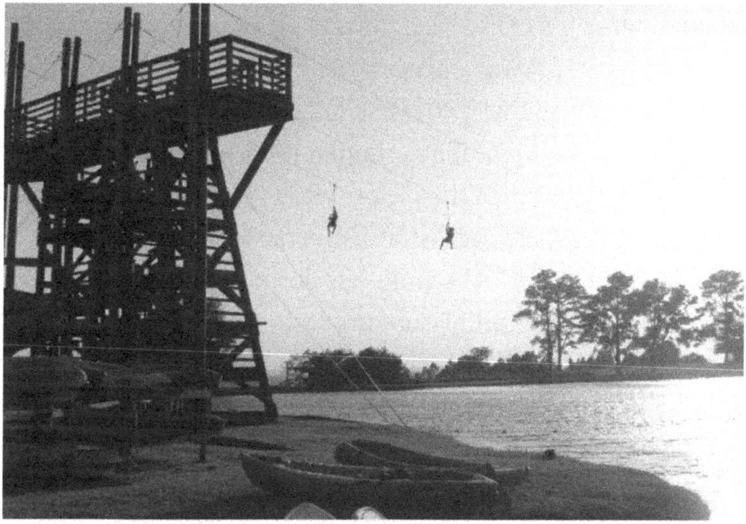

Romancing the Drink

By: Lorraine Gilmore

The small wine glass had been on a shelf in my cupboard for about sixty years. It was only last year that I put it in a yard sale. It was not one that I ever used because it was so small. I still remember the night that I slipped it into my purse. I had gone to the Morton Steakhouse on Mass Ave for dinner with my college roommate at Boston University. The restaurant was only about two blocks from our dorm. It was my first glass of wine, but definitely not my last.

No alcoholic beverages had ever been served in my family home. I had never seen either of my parents take a drink. Daddy kept a bottle of vodka hidden in the bathroom. When he had put in a dropped ceiling, a hole had been left in the tiles for the dangling lightbulb. He could slip a small bottle through the hole and help himself to a drink in secret. He also stopped in at a bar on his way home from work.

When my brother was on leave from the Navy and came home to visit, he kept a cooler of beer in his truck. He would grab a cold one and drink it in the yard. It was only after Daddy died that anyone was allowed to bring their beer into the house. There was never any discussion about either policy, it just seemed to be understood. It was several years later that my brother told me about the hidey hole in the bathroom ceiling.

My second taste of alcoholic beverages was at a beach party on Cape Cod held by the Sailing Club of which I was a member. I drank anything and everything during the hours that we were there and experienced my first black out. I do have a vague memory of being helped back into the dorm and the girls trying to keep me quiet as I sang

"Drunk last night. Drunk the night before. Tonight, I'm going to get drunker than I've ever been before. Singing glorious..."

I was feeling no pain until the next morning arrived with a vicious hangover. One of the other girls in the dorm was kind enough to share a fresh grapefruit which helped with my dehydration. It was the best tasting grapefruit I ever ate.

The years that followed contained no binge drinking. But after being married to an alcoholic for thirteen years, I became a real party girl. I dated a few guys and got drunk quite often. I even did some drunk driving after finishing a night of waiting tables at The Barnside Tavern. One of the benefits was a free drink and we could buy a second one for a dollar. My usual drink was a vodka Stinger. This was a half full brandy snifter of vodka and brandy – very potent. As I drove home, I had to focus carefully because the two yellow lines on the highway seemed to be twisted. I was just lucky that I never got stopped by the state police on that ten-mile drive. It was even luckier that I never had an accident.

I drank more soberly during my second marriage, but as the years passed, I began to binge drink on the weekends. Again, I was lucky to not have any jackpots, as the consequences are called in AA. I never lost a job because of my drinking. I never got arrested for the drunk driving.

In the nineties, I began seeing a therapist. He had previously been a substance abuse counselor and in many of our sessions we would talk about my binge drinking. I remember sitting there with a big smile on my face and saying "I just like to drink." During that time, I was also taking medication for anxiety and depression. I will be forever grateful that when I needed to get a new prescription provider, I made the decision to abstain from drinking alcohol. My thought was there might be a chance that the medication would be more effective if I was sober. Even though the labels on those medication state "do not take with alcohol". I had ignored those instructions.

I stayed clean for about four months until we went on vacation to Tortola. I had never been sober on a vacation and on this one I pulled out all the stops. It was party time once again.

When I returned to another session with my therapist and told him about the vacation binge drinking, he suggested that I try some AA meetings. I am grateful that you can go to AA meetings and skip the self-introduction of "I'm an alcoholic". I was still cruising down the River of Denial. What is interesting to me is that I felt at home in those meetings and was going to about five a week.

After about three months of meetings, we were going to a celebratory lunch and I told myself that I could have a glass of wine. What would that hurt? My husband, his son and I were seated at the table and each of us ordered a glass of wine. The waitress offered to serve us a half bottle with three glasses. Right away my alarm bells went off because I knew that a half bottle contained two and a half glasses of wine – not three. I spoke up and we got a bottle of wine which would give us five glasses.

Somehow after we had lunch, I was able to hear myself and realized that only a person with a drinking problem would have wanted more than the partial glass of wine. I went back to meetings and when I spoke, I would say that I had a problem with alcohol.

"Take the cotton out of your ears and put it in your mouth." That's what the old-timers would tell you. "Just go to meetings and don't drink." I followed their guidance.

That summer I was going to meetings and sat in the same chair at every meeting. Next to me was a guy named

Michael. Whenever he spoke, he would say "my name is Michael and I am an alcoholic". After listening to him for several months, his introduction stuck in my head and I began to accept that I am an alcoholic and that is the introduction I use at meetings.

There was a time that I romanced the drink. I had to use the right glass and went through the motions of savoring the taste of oak or apples. I noticed if the wine had legs – if it was buttery or dry.

There are still times when I think about having another drink. People around me are drinking or ordering a bottle of wine to have with dinner. Just one. What could that hurt? Then I remind myself that one was never enough. It was binge drinking that was fun. I am an alcoholic. I am a binge drinker.

As someone else used to say "I can't drink even if my ass is on fire."

Prompt: thinking of romancing the drink – even though sober for 16 years

"When I was 5 years old, my mother always told me that happiness was the key to life. When I went to school, they asked me what I wanted to be when I grew up. I wrote down 'happy'. They told me I didn't understand the assignment, and I told them they didn't understand life."

- *John Lennon*

Leaning In and Leaning On

By: Suzy Tenenbaum

Leaning in, I put my head on her hind legs.
It's not comfortable, but it's oh so comforting.
Her hair is coarse, but I know that and it's ok.

Taking deep breaths I tell myself to remember this.
Put it in the vault. Click. Put that picture in with other locked memories.
File it under "Most Important."

I stroke her in that spot on the side, by her whiskers, and whisper thank you.
I rub her velvet ears. Petting meditation.

I bow to you my dogi.
That's pronounced doh-gee, hard g.
 It's a combination of dog and yogi, which she is.

Hang on, old dog. Stay with me, beautiful friend.
I need you now more than ever.

The House I Used To Live In

By: John Stickney

I felt the weight of the rubble

the pressures placed

I remember thinking,

"What's the heaviest thing you can imagine?
A house?

It Can Be Done

By: John C. Stipa

I am from a neighborhood where we got into rock fights with the boys on the other side of the railroad tracks.
I don't know why, other than we were taught to despise them.
And then I tossed a football with one of those boys and learned his arm was stronger than mine.

In grade school, I got in a brawl with a boy with black skin.
We each landed punches, neither could call it a win.
When the swinging stopped, and we both bled,
I was surprised to learn that all blood is red.

My teachers steered me away from public high school out of fear of the race riots in the 70's.
But I learned that even private school is not immune.
Hatred must have flunked geography.

In college, I felt an attraction to a beautiful girl who happened to be black, but a "friend" scolded me to perish the thought.
How many guys today would turn down a date with Halle Berry, Beyonce or Jada Pinkett Smith?

In baseball, it was about ability, not ethnicity.
In the business world, it was about character, not color.
I learned successful teams put their best "players" in the positions where their skills did the most good.

When I became a parent, I watched my daughters make friends with kids of many nationalities.
I learned it is not innate for the young to hate.

I've seen that boy with a powerful arm, now a man, take a peaceful knee to teach a life lesson.
Then I see another man use a knee to take a life.
How is he not able to learn?

I was taught differently, but I learned.
It can be done.

Boom!

By: Lee Norman Mehler

Boom!
 The door opens with a rush of air. Two sets of wide eyes are silhouetted by the lightning followed by the first thunder of the young spring season.
 "Come on up here with us," Mother says.
 Brother and Sister scurry across the shag carpeted bedroom at the back of the house. The storm rolled in from the south on their side and propelled them through the maze of toys cluttering the floor. Our bedroom is a refuge this night from the whipping wind and the pelting rain on the metal roof. They jump up with their short legs onto our high four-poster bed. They make it in one leap, pushed from behind by fear. Father raises up the corner of the down comforter to allow Brother and Sister into the soft cave. As Brother and Sister land on the quilted-padding there are static electric sparks like fireflies beneath the billowing sheet. It floats down over the heads and bodies of everyone now safe in the bed.
 "It's funny how the first thunder of the season seems louder than you ever heard before," Father embraces all with his comforting bass voice.
 Brother and Sister shake under the comforter since the house is still chilled from the lingering winter. Their fear accentuates their tremors. Mother hugs Sister and rubs her back.
 "Don't be afraid children," Mother says with a smile. "God must be bowling, and it sounds like he just knocked down all ten pins for a strike."
 "Why does God have to be so loud?" Sister asks.
Brother has on his big brother invincible face.

Mother considers her response because everything to her can be a teaching moment, or an opportunity lost. "Sometimes loud lets you appreciate the beauty of quiet. Otherwise, it would all be the same."

Boom!

"I'm scared too," Brother admits hesitantly.

"Grandfather taught me a trick to get used to the storm gathering around us," Father says.

Boom!

"Now wait for the next lightning flash."

The sky erupts twice and the trees outside move in a dance of white light.

"Now count until you hear the thunder…one, two, three, four, five."

Boom!

"Light moves faster and sound moves slower. Now wait for the next flash." We wait. It strikes.

"And count. One, two, three, four, five, six."

"The storm is moving away," Mother soothes. "The worst is over."

The light continues to quietly explode. Now seven. Now eight. Another flash behind the trees. There is a distance buffer between us and the storm. The volume lessens and the white light fades. A flash and a rumble behind a cloud to the left. Then another to the right.

Sleep overtakes the children.

Mother quietly leaves them in the bed and gently pulls down the shade as the sky lightens slowly on another day.

Their eyes flutter open an hour later. The rising sun peeks around the edge of the shade. Brother pokes Sister and she curls up in a ball.

The water is running down the gutters of the streets. The air smells fresh as the pollen is washed to the drain a block away.

Brother's gray galoshes and Sister's pink boots emerge out of the bench seat at the front door. They hurry to wrap themselves in protective clothing to go outside. The light glistens off their yellow slickers as it breaks between the clouds. Brother and Sister's eyes are wide again as they splash in the remaining puddles from the drama the night before. They count. One, two, three steps.

Again

By: Diane Pascoe

Love is a wonderful thing, as the Michael Bolton song goes.

So, when we met a charming couple, Kevin and Patty, at a dinner on our tour of Scotland, we were thrilled when they told us they were celebrating their second honeymoon.

"How sweet!" I exclaimed, impressed that they loved each other enough to celebrate it one more time.

"No, no," Kevin said. "I mean this *really* is our second honeymoon. We just got married a month ago for the second time. We were first married when we were very young, then we had three kids—we were married for 20 years."

Sounded normal so far.

"Then we split up and divorced. We both re-married other people and stayed married for ten years. During those years apart, Patty and usually bickered when we saw each other, like many divorced couples. But after we both split up with our second spouses, she and I started talking more and getting along well. We soon moved in together. Again."

Patty then jumped into the conversation. "I told Kevin that I thought it was time to get married. Again. So, we did. Our families thought we were nuts, but our kids loved the idea."

I couldn't bring myself to ask for the details of their initial divorce or their second marriages, even though I really wanted to know what happened, but being nosy usually gets me in trouble.

They really are starting over, I thought, noting the sparkling diamond rings on her finger, likely not her original rings from forty years ago. They had come a long way since then.

Although I am not a marriage counsellor, a few red flags went up during our time with this couple. A former policeman, Kevin had retired early at age 50, never to work again— at any job. He chose very supportive wives because Wife 1/3 and Wife 2 both worked until they were 65, while apparently Kevin golfed every day. Hmmm.

I also noted that neither spouse would compromise when deciding where to go for lunch. He wanted pizza, and she didn't. They argued a bit, then went to different restaurants. A couple of hours later we saw them hugging and laughing, so eating lunch together was not critical to their honeymoon happiness.

Every couple has a story, and this couple's story was an unusual one, proving that there is no one way to be happy in love.

I haven't spoken to Patty in many years, but I am sure she and Kevin are still married. They may even be eating lunch together once in awhile.

But who knows? They may have divorced.

Again.

Backyard Tweets

By: Suzy Tenenbaum

<u>1st Tweet</u>

Hey, get off there.
What? I'm sitting here.
Yeah, but that's my spot.
It isn't right now though, is it?
Every day I sit on that spot; it has the best seed.
Why, yes it does. But I'm here now.
Don't you know the rule of first possession?
Yeah, I do, but I don't think that applies here.
I think you've had more than your share.
Fly off and find yourself another perch.
Fly off yourself!

<u>2nd Tweet</u>

They have two feeders now.
Yeah, I saw that.
I still like this one best.
Yeah, me too.
Let the squirrels have that one.
Yeah, those beasts have no manners.
Agreed, such hogs!

3rd Tweet

Here he comes to hang the feeders.
Sometimes it's after 9!
Yeah what's with that?
I think he takes them in so the deer don't eat all the seed overnight.
Well the other day he never brought them out.
Beggars can't be choosers, I guess.
I'm not begging, busking is hard work!

There Is A Storm Coming

By: Terry L. Dismore

Loud disturbance
lightning
flashing
gnashing of limbs
falling to the ground

Hurling winds
clouds bursting
water rising
clamoring noises

There is a storm coming

Rabbits, butterflies, foxes and other
terrestrial animals burrow
underground, seeking shelter in trees,
under rocks or leaves

There is a storm coming

Where to hide
What to do
Who to call
fear dominating us all

There is a storm coming

Challenge the storms
that come your way
stand flat footed
strong
face the storms

It's merely the cost of living
life each and everyday

Hold hands together
remembering collectively we
are strong in the mist of the storm

There is a storm coming!

At The Museum

By: Claudia Blanchard

We rush past the busts
Of the ancients
Broken noses, cold marble eyes
Staring at no one
Rulers of none

We want to view the contemporary exhibit
A mash-up of Banksy and Basquiat
Of Harig and Kusama

Shelve the classics
History is history
Shove Socrates to the science department
Shift Plato to philosophy
Bury Aristotle in the art curriculum
Toss Hadrian to the humanities
Wait, that department has been
ransacked too

My face is wet
With tears from
Rita Mae, Toni, Lynn and Willa.

Old Friends

By: Lorraine Gilmore

Caroline stared at the menu board at Chick-fil-A, wondering why she bothered. She always ordered the Spicy Deluxe Chicken Sandwich; Katherine usually got the Chick-n Strips and Alice got the Cool Wrap followed up with a Frosty Lemonade. They often talked about skipping the entrees and getting Cookies and Cream Milkshakes. But so far it was just talk.

    The three of them had been meeting there every Friday as long as they had been neighbors which was about four years. Katherine was next to arrive.

    "Hi, is Alice saving us a table?"

    "Alice isn't able to meet with us today."

    "She's usually the first one here, what's up?"

    "You haven't heard?"

    "I just got back from a visit with my grandkids in Boone. What did I miss?"

    "Alice fell earlier this week when she stepped off the curb at the Dollar Tree. She's okay, but she skinned her knee and is sore all over."

    "So, she's not coming today?"

    "No. I think she's a little depressed because the doctor said it's time for her to get a walker."

    "I can't blame her. I'd be depressed too at that thought." As she said this, Katherine tried to swallow a laugh.

    "What's so funny?"

    "I'm thinking about Alice's cocker spaniel. Georgie can be a little hard to handle, I can just see her trying to walk him trailing behind with her walker."

"I guess you stifled yourself because it's really not funny."

"No, it's not and neither is what all of us are facing. Every time I spoke with my sister-in-law, she would say 'Getting old ain't for sissies' and she was so right."

"I know. I try not to think about what awaits us down the road. I'm sure that my reaction time is not what it used to be. Every time I pull into the garage, I'm grateful that I've had no problems driving."

"I'm really grateful that I am still in good health," Katherine said as she knocked on wood.

"Me, too. Still, it seems that my appointment book has really changed."

"What do you mean?"

"It seems to fill up with doctor visits and trips to the physical therapist."

"There's another difference too."

"What's that?"

"There was a time when our social life centered around weddings and baby showers. Lately I've been going mostly to funerals."

Caroline let out a big sigh. "Yeah, so many of my high school classmates have died. I'm always thankful for another day above the grass."

"Me, too," Katherine said. "Well, shall we table this depressing discussion and order our food?"

"Sounds good to me. Maybe this is the day we skip the healthier stuff and just have their frozen lemonade or a milkshake."

"I'm with you. Let's do it."

Prompt: the other day I saw a neighbor walking her dog and she was trailing behind with her walker

Sorry

By: John Stickney

As someone who is thinking of one day aspiring to a higher political office, right now I am a board member of the Meadow Park Landscaping Committee, which my handlers assure me is the right place for me to be for now, so, as someone with higher aspirations, I feel, judging by the current political and social climate, that it is time for me to get a few things out in front of the public.

I'm sorry. I'm really, truly sorry.

I'm sorry mom that I never picked up after myself or maintained my room in the manner you requested.

I'm sorry that I copied off of Jimmy McKrakin's spelling paper in the 5th grade, specifically unit 12, in which Jimmy misspelled the word "impossible." I'm sorry that I did not copy off of Annie Sabotka's paper; she never, ever misspelled a word in her life.

I'm sorry that when my High School football coach wasn't looking, I dogged it during my penalty laps. I'm sorry that during summer two-a-day football practices I wanted to drink water and refused to chew the mandatory salt tablets thus evidencing my bad attitude and causing the aforementioned penalty laps to be imposed. Coach, if I hadn't dogged it, if I had just eaten those salt tablets, I know that I'd be a better man today.

I'm sorry that I thought it was funny when my brother fell off his bike while trying to impress Barbara Velocast by riding with no hands. I'm sorry that the memory of this still cracks me up today.

I'm sorry, really sorry that I used Roger Maris and not Fred Whitfield's rookie card in my wheel spokes.

I'm sorry that I forgot to vote in three presidential elections. But you can hardly blame me, once every four years, come on.

I'm sorry, really sorry, that I look at cleavage as if the mystery of life is between there, waiting to be revealed. I'm sorry that on some level I still believe it truly is.

I'm sorry for all the lies, all of them, even the ones you haven't discovered yet and especially the ones that I haven't yet said.

I'm sorry that when asked by my wife, during our second pregnancy, after being woken from a sound sleep, at three in the morning, for the second night in the row, for a series of "these might be them contractions" late in the third trimester - when asked by my wife what I was thinking about, I'm sorry, truly sorry, that I told her the truth.

This I'm sorry goes to my children - you know that college fund all your Christmas and birthday money goes into, well, I'm sorry to tell you that the Easter Bunny used it to finance the next five Easters.

To the IRS, I'm sorry you caught me.

I'm sorry I told that policeman that in my state there are left turn on red laws. And I'm sorry, really sorry that he still gave me a ticket.

I'm sorry that I ignored my broker when he told me to buy bread at 50 cents a loaf. If only I had listened, I'd be a rich man today.

I'm sorry I bought that Macarena record on CD and made it my ringtone. I'm sorry that I cannot figure out how to undo my ringtone and too cheap to buy a new phone.

I'm sorry that I never return my phone calls or leave a message after the beep.

I'm sorry for all this and much, much more.

Truly sorry. Filled with remorse. Believe me when I tell you it won't happen again

I'm sorry. Really truly sorry. Believe me when I tell you the buck stops here.

I'm sorry. So sorry. And let me conclude by saying that I'm really, truly sorry.

Now, forgive me and let's get on with life.

But first, does anyone want to buy a certified, preowned Macarena CD?

Leaving

By: Lee Norman Mehler

The memories wash over her like multiple waves at the shore when caught by one and blindsided by another, closer than expected. It almost knocks her off your feet. But she stiffens and resists the sway of the salt water. They hold hands as the mist rolls in overtaking everything. She feels his grip loosen and she grab tighter to compensate.

***

Months later, she could have left. There was no reason, no logic, just instinct. He had given her one last chance. He begged her to go. She hesitated.

"You know how there are moments in your life that are etched in your mind forever?" she asked him.

He barely said anything. "Yeah, I guess." Almost inaudible.

"When it becomes so clear and certain that there is no question, no doubt?" she continued.

"What?" he mumbled toward the wall.

"I just had one of those." She hesitated. "You said go and I didn't. I'm not leaving, I'm not. No matter how much you push me away."

A tear started falling, but she stayed in the shadows so he could not see. "No matter what you say I can't leave you. No matter how mean you act, I know it is a lie, not real." She had her doubts, but she was determined to hide it. "This is not like the last time. I won't run and hide. You need me and I still need you."

She thought she saw him flinch, but she wasn't sure. He emitted a low moan, and she froze. He shuddered and she could feel his pain without touching him. He didn't like to be touched any more. She wanted to remember, for both of them.

This was the last time he would say her name.

"Joanne, I'm scared."

"I know, I know. I will be here forever. If you don't see me, recognize me, I promise I will be here for both of us."

Then he went silent, and the fog enveloped his world.

***

A year later he is not really here anymore. She shows him photos of that last trip to Costa Rica. He smiles, but looks somewhere past the page of the dogeared photo book to another world. His eyes are vacant again.

She looks down at the photo album and that will have to be enough.

They say it's harder on the caregiver. She had no idea until left alone, in the same room with him. He had always been there when she needed him. Now it was her turn.

"We'll always have the beach at Puntarenas, Tom." She is accustomed to talking and getting no response. She still holds out hope. He is happy now in his own world, stuck in that moment on the beach. She can still feel the warmth and pressure of his hand in hers that day. The last thing he remembers are the Scarlet Macaws high in the tree-tops. Their loud cries let them know they are there before they spot them.

She stands now looking south with her arm lightly caressing his shoulder. The clouds part slightly, and the rays of the sun dance off the dust in the air as it falls slowly to the ground.

"It's time to go, Joanne," the nurse says softly.

She leaves the brightly lit room saying, "See you tomorrow, dear."

His back is to her, leaning on his cane, staring directly into the sun.

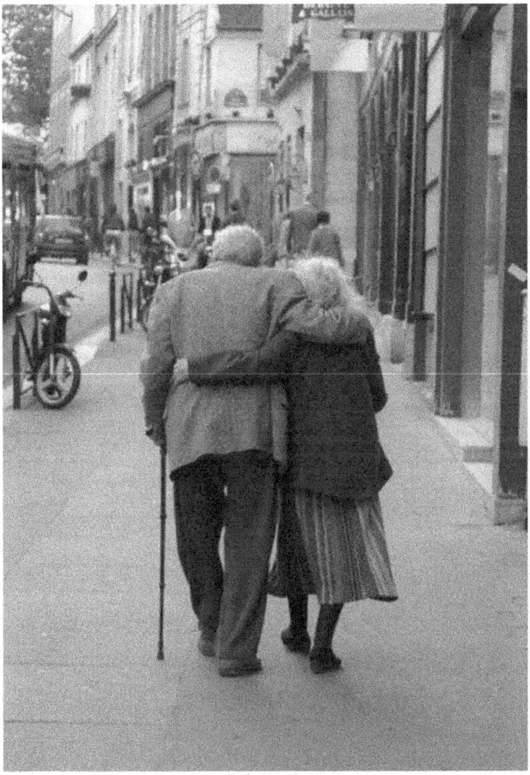

Endurance

By: Barbara Dullaghan

Pieces of shells left behind
On an expansive beach
Just as years of acquaintances
Are left across the miles
Only a few remain whole
Surviving the turmoil of the sea,
Surviving the crashing and pounding,
Surviving the rough and tumble of life's challenges.
Life-long friends and family
Continue to support and share their love
Whole but with imperfections
Just like me.

A Vessel Not Only A Vase

By: Terry L. Dismore

The morning sun burst through the clouds greeting and declaring the perfect day to not only be a **Vase, but a Vessel**

Inner yearnings to rub shoulders with the human race
family dinners
handshakes
hugs
kisses
laughter of children gliding through the air
playing without a care

Mothers in their aprons, hanging clothes on the line
telling stories, watching their kids
knowing the secret that kids, are just kids
and the importance of being a **Vessel not only a Vase**

The witness of a single blade of grass on the hill
where the purple poppy lilacs live
trees bending
enjoying the sea mist
compliments of the wind

Strong emotions of **anger, fear and hate**
not welcome in my **Vase**
and certainly not in my **Vessel**

"Life is really simple, but we insist on making it complicated."
- *Confucius*

Don't Give Up

By: Diane Pascoe

It was a very tough week for everyone. Nothing seemed to go smoothly.

The surgery to drain the abscess on Mom's right buttock had gone well on Saturday, although I'm still not sure why it took a week to diagnose the abscess when she had been complaining to everyone for days that her bum hurt.

Post-surgery, the nursing home staff regularly cleaned the surgical opening, but Mom didn't like the wound touched. In protest, she smacked one staff member, then another, then another, with her skinny, toothpick arms. Luckily, they ignored her behavior.

The next day, while Mom was in the bathroom, my sister Janet sat on the edge of Mom's hospital bed, but when she stood up, she set off an alarm. A recorded voice said over and over, "Do not get out of bed!" so Janet sat frozen on Mom's bed until a swat team arrived to wrangle Mom back into her bed. Everything is complicated in our little Mom's life.

On Monday, two days after her surgery, Mom was able to return to the nursing home, but a few things had changed while she was away. A Russian lady at Mom's dining table who always groaned while eating, much to Mom's disgust, had died two days earlier while Mom was in the hospital. No family, no visitors. Gone, as though she had never been there.

On Tuesday morning, Janet pushed Mom in a wheelchair down the hall past a much younger man on her floor who had been severely injured in a motorcycle accident.

"I hate him" Mom grumbled.

"Mom, please try to be kinder to people," said Janet.

"I'll try, but I can't promise anything," Mom muttered. At least she was honest.

Many things annoy her. The masks on the staff and visitors make Mom crazy. She doesn't recognize people under their masks, nor can she hear them well with their mouths covered. And a particular staff member doesn't talk to her at all when she's helping her.

"Why don't you ever talk to me?" Mom asked her. No response, just silence. Mom hates being ignored and invisible. Who doesn't?

The next day, when Janet arrived at the nursing home, the first thing she had to do was to clean Mom up. She put Mom's bottom denture in, brushed her hair, and washed off the chocolate pudding that was on her face. She was able to restore Mom to factory condition except for the 93 years of patina proudly gracing her skin.

Janet then went to say hello to the man cross the hall, only to hear Mom bellow in a voice that would wake the dead.

"Where are you, Janet?"

Mom couldn't see Janet across the hall because she had lost her glasses, and she can't eat or see anyone without them. Her glasses were nowhere to be found in the hospital—not in her clothing pockets, her bed, her pajamas nor in her drawers, so Janet urgently ordered new glasses. Everything has gone missing in the nursing home it seems—her wheelchair, her clothes, and her glasses, but also her appetite, her manners, and her mind. This is life at 93.

But Mom has moments of clarity too in which she shows insight and understanding. Recently she said, "I know I need a lot of care because I can't do anything for myself anymore. I know how hard it must be for everyone but please don't give up on me."

Don't worry Mom. We won't give up if you don't.

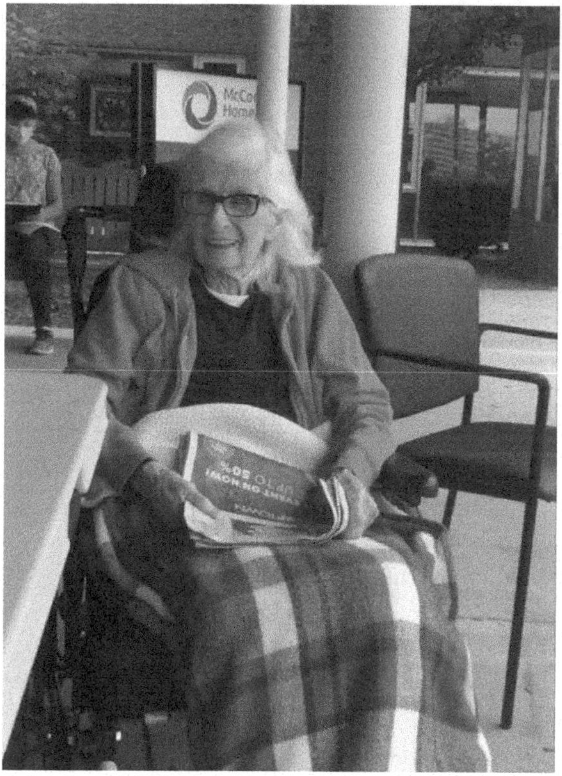

Blue Beautiful Blue

By: Suzy Tenenbaum

I have a thing for blue
That's an understatement
I'm in this lifelong
love affair with blue

Blue speaks to me
It encourages me to be joyful
Yet it also accepts all my feelings

It's okay to be blue

Sometimes it sings to me
Tea for two and two for tea
Me for blue and blue for me

Blue grabs my attention
It brightens my day
If you are wearing blue
I will be noticing you

Blue lived inside of me
In the eyes of my three babies
It will always be a part of me

Blue lowers my heart rate
It settles me down

The shades of blue are varied as to meet every mood
 Or to energize or be inspirational

There is stately, mature, sometimes serious navy blue
Young and fresh baby blue
Cornflower blue
Cerulean, that lovely shade of blue ranging between azure and darker sky blue
Teal, turquoise, and periwinkle
Royal blue, aqua, and sapphire
Steel blue, cobalt blue and electric blue

These blues mingle amiably in my closet
Just as I get along with all the members of the blue family

At the end of each day I lay my head down
On a sea of baby blue
Peaceful and welcoming
It eases me into sleep

Put a blue quilt on me when I lay dying and
When I'm gone I'll be up in the boundless beautiful blue skies

Eternally blue
Loving you

Thou Shalt Not Kill

By: Claudia Blanchard

And yet,
Shotguns
Pistols
Revolvers
Machine guns
Handguns
Submachine guns
Battle rifles
Semi-automatic rifles
Muskets
Pump action
Sniper rifles
Carbines
Break action
Assault rifles
Long guns
Automatic rifles
Semi-automatic pistols
What to do with so many arms?
Asks the *Bodhisattva*.

The Train

By: Lee Norman Mehler

I must preface this by saying I really love my wife. No, it's not just a habit, or taken for granted. Our life together is multifaceted. Almost spiritual. Emotions now resemble a calm, placid lake with no ripples. A sun slowly rising and warming the top of my now bare head. There are conversations that continue into the night beyond any explanation. We have moments of silence that extend into an hour of solitude even when we are in the same room. We are comfortable in each other's wordless presence. Passion still happens, less frequently with less spontaneity than when we were younger. Life is good.

So why do I keep noticing the woman with cascading red hair on the 8:15 morning train to New York City from Princeton Junction? I first spotted her on the platform as we waited for the express a week ago. She tries to keep warm as the wind whips through the canyon between the billboards and the overcrowded plexiglass shelters. Her tartan skirt lifts slightly in the tumult of the stiff breeze. In the distance there is a high-pitched whistle of the approaching train right on time as usual. It arrives with an additional rush of air to urge us into the warmth of the commuter car, with standing room only.

She is offered a seat by a young stud with a two-day beard, wireless earbuds and a cap worn the wrong way. She refuses to sit down and sways with the jostling of the train as it speeds toward the city with the rhythmic clip-clip-clip of the tracks beneath. Her weight shifts from one foot to the other. She must be a dancer or aspires to be one.

Last week, when the train took a curve too fast, she temporarily lost her footing. She quickly caught herself and glanced momentary at me. It was not long enough to let me see the color of her eyes. I imagine they're green.

She never smiles, but she isn't frowning either. Kind of like the Mona Lisa after a few beers on a Friday night. Her expression seems to always be on the verge of changing, but never quite getting there.

My eyes roll up to the advertisements above the windows as the suburban landscape blurs by. This is my usual head motion to disguise my staring. My gaze falls again to the soft curves of her body, only slightly hidden by the middle weight, knee high coat to keep out the autumn chill. I appreciate fine art and the lines of elegance of the human figure that inspire the masters' brush strokes. Some people are more visually stunning. They beg to be painted. I imagine what is hidden by her coat and her downward gaze.

But I'm afraid. Not of violating my relationship with my wife because I don't think I would do anything except talk. But it has been so long since I have exposed myself to any new relationship. And I feel that even friendship may be a violation of some sanctity. So, my mind wanders and wonders what could be, knowing that I am set in my ways and too afraid of life, or changes in life, to take a chance.

We approach the city as the conductor announces our destination in a muffled tone that is hard to decipher. My mind races as the pace of the train slows with the space between the rails increasing with every inch forward. As we enter the tunnel under the river the landscape goes dark and engulfs the train in blackness.

The dreams of what could be dim with the light.

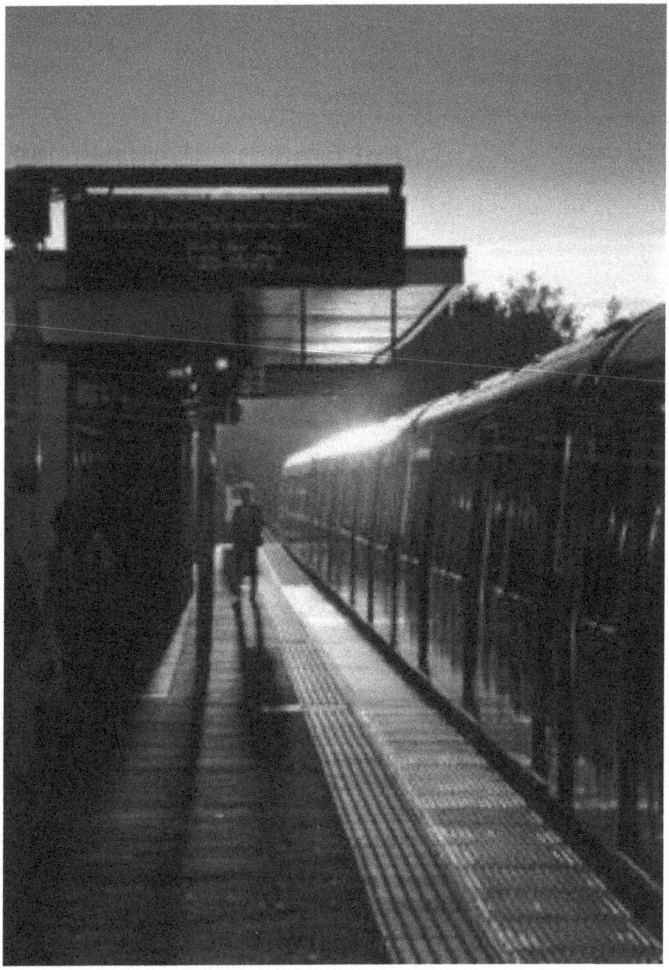

Summer's Edge

By: John Stickney

Too hot
To sleep in the daytime
Too many animals stirring
To sleep at night
What will the moon do?

Waiting for the Wife

By: Lorraine Gilmore

It's a bright, sunny day in early June. There's very little wind, and no humidity. The grass is green and the birds are singing. A perfect day for a game of golf. Yet here I sit ... inside, in a store, waiting for the wife. At least I'm sitting in a comfortable chair. The store has quite a few comfortable chairs in each department and I'm sure they are all full of others, just like me, who are waiting for their wife.

Just wish I had a book to read.

Every time I end up going on one of these shopping trips, I wonder why I came along. I never went in a store to get new clothes and took more than twenty minutes. She has to try on many blouses or skirts and go look in the mirror and then try on some more. Why is it so difficult for her to make up her mind?

Here she comes again.

"Honey, what do you think? Does this dress make me look fat?"

Do I look stupid? That question is a minefield. Are there any words that men hate more than those? Well, maybe no one wants to hear the words "we need to talk".

After forty years, this should not feel so hard. After so much time, you would think that she would just leave me in peace! Besides, she has already formed her own opinion. What I say will not make any difference in her decision. And, her feelings get hurt so easily. I always try to say the right thing, but it never ends up very good.

"George? Are you listening to me?"

"I'm sorry dear. Did you say something?"

"Do you think that this dress makes me look fat?"

"You know, Margaret, you're as lovely as ever and that shade of green has always been your favorite."

"But, does it make me look fat?"

Why can't she just leave it alone? No matter what I say she will buy the one that she wants. I wish this weren't so hard! I've always been a good husband and tagged along on these shopping trips. I always take her out to lunch when we finish. We have a good meal and enjoy each other's company. If only she would leave me out of this.

"Margaret, it looks lovely on you and you're as lovely as the day I married you."

"Oh, George! You say the sweetest things! I'm so glad that you like it. It will only take a few minutes for me to change. I have another one that I'd like you to see."

As she returned to the fitting room, George put his head in his hands.

God must really be a woman to put us through this kind of misery. I really need to find a way to avoid these shopping trips without hurting her feelings. I'm not sure I know how I will do that. She really expects me to come along after all these years.

Maybe next time I'll say that I forgot that I was going to meet up with Bob that day. She'd understand that I can't disappoint my best friend. I'm sure that I can count on him to back me up when I explain. I'll bet that he has to go on shopping trips with his wife. Maybe we can help each other out.

"Honey, what do you think of this one?"

Thank goodness! She didn't ask the fat question. But, what do I say about it? I don't know the first thing about women's fashion.

"That shade of blue almost matches the color of your eyes. It's very flattering."

"I'm so glad that you like it. I think that I'll get both of them."

She took a few steps and turned around.

"George? Would you like to stop in the men's department and we can pick out some new shirts for you?"

Oh, God, please! She always wants to pick out those pansy colors like pink or lavender.

"That's awfully sweet, Margaret. But not today. I'm hungry. Let's go to lunch and I can look for shirts another time."

"If you say so, dear. I'll be right back."

Thank you, Jesus! A good steak and a strong Manhattan will make up for all of this misery!

Woke Up This Morning

By: Terry L. Dismore

Where is the land of the free and the home of the brave?
or was that simply a fairy-tale or myth?

Virus killing thousands,
mass graves not enough of a disgrace

I woke up this morning
expecting to be on the good planet earth

Martin Luther King Jr. didn't die in vain
Maya said, "When you learn, teach"
I doubt she meant hate

Mother Theresa lived a life of humanity for all
Einstein, George Washington Carver, Marie Curie
dedicated lives of service, was it all in vain?

Kennedy cried, "Ask not what your country can do for you,
but what you can do for your country!"

Woke up this morning confused and wondering
was I still on the good **Planet Earth**?

That Damned Owl

By: Barbara Dullaghan

When my husband and I moved our family of five from New York to a suburb of Grand Rapids, Michigan, I knew there were things I would miss. My parents, the hustle and bustle of the state, my friends and the Hudson River. What I did not realize I would long for was Wise Potato Chips.

Yes, I said, looong for. I missed that salty, crispy chip so much that, on my trips back home, I would stuff the little green and yellow bags with the yellow owl eye into my luggage to covet when I returned to Michigan. I did not share, nor did anyone realize that I brought them home. It's no wonder I developed health problems fifteen years later.

Wise Potato Chips have long evoked childhood memories of finding a shady tree and sharing a snack and Coke with my best friend, Margie. Delving into the company's history, I discovered this is their 100th anniversary. No wonder I am still hooked; that chip has literally been tempting me my entire life!

Nowadays, websites tout that my favorite chip is gluten free, with no MSG, 0g trans-fat, and no preservatives. But the reviews report that the taste is not the same as the chips of old. Nor does it have that crisp for your crunch. Too oily!

During years of travel around the world, I actually have stopped in my tracks upon seeing Wise Potato Chips in store aisles. I stop, look, and my face scrunches up deep in thought. *Do I long for those? Do I want them? Is that wise owl on the package mocking me?*

I'm happy to report that, most of the time, I choose a healthier snack, but always with a twinge of regret. I dare say the chips were intertwined with a lot of issues. I think my second therapist helped me figure that out.

With my next therapist, I hope to discover why the chips in the Pringles can are so damned orderly and how do I deal with the portability of shoestring potatoes in a can?

The Collar

By: Diane Pascoe

When Honey takes our furry grand pup, Murphy, for long walks, he usually puts his harness on him because Murph is a strong boy who pulls hard. But if it's a short walk, his regular collar is fine— or at least it would be if I could find it. The last place I saw the collar was on the porch coffee table. It had been lying there for three days, ever since Murph came to see us for a little vacay from his parents, Braden and Taylor. Then yesterday the collar disappeared from the coffee table.

That collar is our son Braden's favourite because it is decorated with logos of the Toronto Maple Leafs and he is a die-hard Leafs fan. So, I knew one thing for sure: Murph could not go home without that collar. I would have asked Honey if he'd seen it, but he had gone fishing, so I fired off a text to him.

In the meantime, I tried to imagine where Honey would put the collar if he moved it from the table. I checked the mudroom baskets, bins and bench, as well as the front hall table basket loaded with leashes, and poop bags. I looked in the garage and bathrooms, then looked under the sofas, chairs, and tables. No blue collar.

Beads of sweat glistened on my forehead because I knew that Murph was a dogman who loved to keep on a schedule. He would soon be whimpering for me to get moving, but I had to focus on finding his collar first.

Ding! A text from Honey: "The last time I saw the collar, Murph was wearing it."

Good lord—this man is no help at all. If Murph were wearing the collar I wouldn't be looking everywhere for it, now would I?

As I pondered my next step in this exhaustive search, Murph sauntered onto the porch from his sleeping spot in the bedroom, looking at me expectantly with his big brown eyes.

"Murph," I said to my canine grandchild, "what are we going to do about your collar?" Suddenly, as he turned his head slightly to look out the window, a ring of faded blue Maple Leafs peeked through his long, blonde neck hair. The collar. Right where Honey said.

As they say, you always find a lost item in the last place you look.

I will never live this down.

An Unexpected Kindness

By: Diane Pascoe

One Sunday evening many years ago, I flew to Louisville, Kentucky from Raleigh, NC. I didn't need a rental car as I would only be at a conference center for a training course for two days and then at the Marriott Hotel in the evenings. I preferred to take the airport shuttle to the hotel, and just grab a taxi the next morning to go to the conference center for the workshop.

I had been looking forward to this two-day course recommended by my boss, the CEO of our company. Good enough for me.

Early Monday morning, I made my way to the hotel front desk. I didn't know how far it would be to the conference center so I thought I would leave early just to be safe.

"Good morning," I said to the young man at the desk. "I'm going to the Louisville Conference Center for a workshop this morning. Could you please call me a cab?"

"Sure," he said. "I'll let you know when you can expect the taxi to arrive – can you just wait over there for a few minutes?"

I stood off to the side of the desk as I observed the clerk on the phone making some calls. I checked my watch to make sure I would not be late. No problem.

The clerk hung up the phone. I immediately knew something had gone wrong by his sombre face. I felt a slight uneasiness when he approached.

"Ma'am, I'm so sorry but there are no taxis available anywhere in Louisville right now. There is a big event at the University which starts later this morning, so all the taxis have been assigned to the airport to pick up attendees. It will be a couple of hours before anyone is available to take you to the conference center."

"But my workshop starts in less than an hour and I can't be late. I don't know how far it is — do you think I can get there on time if I walk?"

"No chance," the clerk said. "You can only get there from here by highway and it's too dangerous to walk."

"This is a nightmare!" I moaned. I'd come all the way to Louisville for this course only to miss the whole morning? What a waste of time! I stood there, paralyzed by indecision.

The young clerk looked as worried as I felt. "Excuse me. I'll be right back," he said and stepped into the back room behind the desk. He emerged a minute later.

"Ma'am, I will drive you to the conference center. My car is right near the back door, so I'll just grab my keys and we'll be on our way. My manager will take over the desk while I'm gone."

I was stunned. This young man had taken ownership of my problem that seemed to have no solution. I followed him down the hall to the back door of the hotel and jumped into the passenger seat of his car. In ten minutes, we arrived at the workshop venue– with time to spare! I thanked the young man profusely and handed him a gratuity which he declined.

When I returned to the hotel by taxi later that day, I thanked the manager for letting the desk clerk take me to the workshop. I did not expect such kindness.

That night, I went on the Marriott website to send a note of commendation to the hotel, letting them know that they hired a fine young man as well as a manager who put their customers first. I don't think driving a customer to a workshop is one of a desk clerk's job duties, but he jumped into action and saved the day for me.

I have often thought about that experience and how grateful I felt to the desk clerk for his thoughtfulness and initiative. I hope life has rewarded him well.

By the way, the workshop turned out to be the best I have ever attended.

Time Lock

By: John Stickney

Perhaps your idea of a failing present - "Now where did I put those keys?" or "In what row did I park the car at the big box store?" is not a case of memory loss or cognitive wear. It is more likely an incident of TEMPORAL DISPLACEMENT.

Memory loss is always a fall back position, the "go to" for family, friends, colleagues, etc. and everyday happenstances and common situations. Heck, it is a staple of jokes for any "aged" character in situation comedies and other popular entertainment programming. Thus the idea of cognitive slippage is reinforced on a daily basis.

But what if that's not the true state of things?

Physicists associated with research at that Hadron Collider have demonstrated observable phenomenon known as "TEMPORAL DISPLACEMENT" or, as we might call it in popular parlance - TIME TRAVEL. Among their discoveries were mice, seconds, minutes older on a molecular level. Steam from coffee far less steamy. Cold beverages degrees warmer, with dissipated ice cube patterns. All observed and documented. All observed, documented and replicated. Because The Large Hadron Collider (CERN) is the world's largest and most powerful particle accelerator, scientist wondered if this phenomenon was isolated to only the neutrinos and other particles within a field generated by the collider. Again, rigorous testing was performed outside the said field, in adjacent office and laboratory. Starling, the results were the same.

Mice older, check.

Less steamy steam, check.

Warming cold and melting ice, check and check.

Just listen to the testimony of Dr. Hans Gruber: "We were sitting and talking over a cuppa, and time, we noted, went so quickly, it went lickety-splitly. It was most unusual."

Working day and night and in the extra moments allowed by the extra time travel, the scientist were able to counter the effect of TEMPORAL DISPLACEMENT. "Harnessing the means to travel through time," Dr. Gruber noted, "proved to a logistical impossibility with our current level of technology. But arresting time, stopping one's displacement, well that was achievable." Those scientists are working on the collider, are all wearing the TIME LOCK device developed by Dr. Gruber and his team of time stoppers. Particle acceleration is an incredibly expensive process, even one missing moment can add up to millions of dollars very quickly. Now, they have ensured no more moments will be lost.

The good news is the same TIME LOCK device developed and worn by these brave scientists is available for sale to us, the public. Designed to clip to one's belt, no bigger that an old-style pager, this device is 100% money back guaranteed to stop your personal TEMPORAL DISPLACEMENT. Three easy payments of $29.99, shipping included, and you will never have to look for your car keys or car again.

The first forty orders in the next hour also receive a complementary Hadron Collider Mug. It is guaranteed to keep the cold cold, the hot hot, and time ever present.

Pick up that phone, don't waste any more time, call today, 800-864-3928.
Put time back on your side where it belongs.
Order your TIME LOCK today.

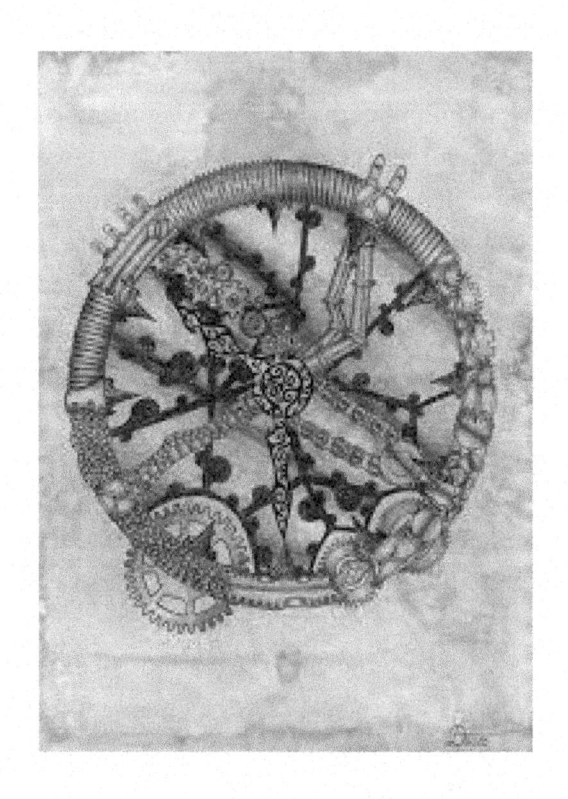

Celebrate Earth Day

By: Claudia Blanchard

Do you like adventure?
Make Planet Earth your next vacation destination!
We have so many atrocities to offer
You and your family.

Turn up the heat with our
Western Drought and Forest Fire package.
Watch colorful flames destroy
Acres of forest!

If you prefer something wet and wild
Consider our *Southern Hurricane* adventure.
Here you can experience torrential rainfall
And floods.
Watch Earthlings as they climb to their roofs
Crying for help.
This is the best water park in the universe.
Warning – dogs do drown.

For enthusiasts of destruction
Experience *The Majesty of The Wind*.
See swaths of neighborhoods destroyed.
Feel the wind in your hair
But be mindful of flying debris.

Call your Universal Travel Agent.
Come visit Planet Earth.
This offer won't last much longer.

My Super Power

By: Lorraine Gilmore

Were you ever embarrassed by a teacher? Did you feel so humiliated in front of your classmates that you just wanted to drop through the floor and disappear? When that happened to me in the fourth grade, Mrs. Thomas and I were both in for a big surprise.

"Mary Margaret Johnson! Where do you think you are? Were you raised in a barn? Take your finger out of your nose this minute!"

I was gobsmacked! You may not know what that means, but neither do I. But it sounds good, doesn't it?

I was also very angry.

"Go to the black board this instant and write I will not pick my nose 100 times."

I got up from my desk feeling like my shoes were filled with cement. As I plodded by Mrs. Thomas, I noticed her shiny black shoes. I wished right then and there that they were filled with thousands of sharp nails.

Right away she let out the most horrible scream.

The whole class and I were astonished to see that there were thousands of sharp nails poking through her shoes into her feet.

I never had to go to the blackboard and write those words and Mrs. Thomas never came back to teach in our school.

The next time this sort of thing happened to me was in fifth grade. I was out on the playground at recess and Mary Alice Grainger pushed me off the swing. She dared to do this because she was a year older than me and a lot bigger.

As I fell into the dirt, I wished that she would fall off the swing and skin her knees. A few minutes after she began to swing, that very thing happened.

I stood there with my mouth open for a few seconds and then decided to put this to a test. I looked at Mary Alice and wished that she would fall into a very deep hole. Sure enough, a few minutes later the ground fell away from her until she lay in a ten-foot hole. As she lay there screaming her head off, I went to get our teacher. After Mrs. O'Brien came out to see this for herself, she called the fire department. They put a large ladder down the hole and brought her up. Mary Alice never came back to our school.

I never told anyone about what I had done. I knew that they either would not believe me or I would be in a lot of trouble. Somehow, I knew I needed to be careful with this newfound ability and over the years I have used my superpower only a few times.

I'm telling you about this because of what happened at the airport this morning.

My husband and I were sitting at the gate, waiting for our plane to arrive so that we could board for our flight to Charlotte. The man sitting to my right had his cell phone in his hands. I could see that there was a video displayed with some woman who was talking on and on. Even though it was loud and annoying, her words were not clear to me. I like silence. I find cell phone noise very annoying. "I wish his cell phone would melt." The words were in my thoughts before I could even think about what would happen.

The next thing I knew, the man was screaming. I looked over and saw that his cell phone had twisted into an unrecognizable shape. There was no way that it could ever be repaired. He grabbed his carry-on bag and ran off.

I have no idea where he was going. I just sat there and enjoyed the silence as I waited for the boarding announcement.

I need to be more careful with my thoughts especially when I'm angry.

The prompt for this was the man in the airport on May 1st using his cellphone as we waited for our flight to Charlotte.

Quiet

By: Terry L. Dismore

Sit in the quiet
think see and do in the quiet
reflections & revelations
reveled in the quiet

Void
evacuation
of the heart and soul
found and meet you in the quiet

In the quiet you
know who you are
which way to go
and what to do next

Emptying
becomes fullness
darkness becomes
shimmering beams of light
roots take hold and grow
doubts become hope
knowing it will be alright

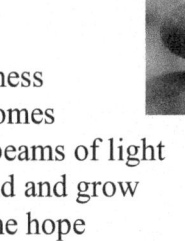

In the quiet the soul meets the
seeing eye to the universe

In the quiet of the night we become one!

"I've learned that people will forget what you said, people will forget what you did, but people will never forget how you made them feel."
- *Maya Angelou*

SADness My Old Friend

By: John C. Stipa

Hello SADness my old friend,
You've come to visit me again.

By friends I'm supposedly surrounded,
Like an ocean wraps an island I'm not hounded.
I know my voice makes a sound when I speak,
Do the on switches for ears need a tweak?

I think my S.O.S. is clear and sonic
But isn't that just so ironic?
That I resort to Morse code
When Instagram or Twitter is the mode.

They may as well go home,
I'm better when alone.
No one wishes to engage those who are down,
Unlike them, SADness, you always come around.

Failure is like air,
It is quite literally, everywhere.
What I do, say, think, or make,
somehow, it's all a mistake,
I breathe it in, accustomed to the ache.

Does a light exist to lift me out of these depths?
Oh, please shine it onto salvation's steps!
I desperately need hope,
SADness, I'm at the end of my rope.

But I fear your teeth have bitten deep,
Making my climb too steep.
Will I pass away, down in this pit of despair?
Or will something save me, does anyone care?

SADness, my constant companion, I hope I offend,
Leave me now, and send a true friend.

Lucky Duck

By: Suzy Tenenbaum

I don't know what makes a duck lucky
Maybe if the pond is clean and the turtles don't get in their way
Maybe if they score a horde of tasty insects
Or hap upon a shiny object, then they are a lucky duck

But I can tell you what it means to me to be a lucky duck
It's waking up every day and the first thing I see is his face
The first thing I touch is his arm
Then at night I thank my lucky stars, whatever those are

I don't know what makes a star lucky
But that one shining so brightly last night
As we strolled hand in hand
I'm sure that was a lucky star shining on this lucky duck

The Recipe

By: Lee Norman Mehler

I remember baking with my mother when I was young before the real world took up much of my day. She patiently guided my hands to interlace the strips of flattened dough to create the basket weave covering the thin cut granny smith apple slices. She opened the oven door and a wave of dry heat rolled over us. As the pie cooked, the sweet aroma of fresh baked love overwhelmed the house.

We stood side by side at the kitchen island, slowly rolling and punching down the ingredients for the challah. After showing me how to braid it together, we slid it into the preheated 375-degree oven for forty-five minutes where it eventually turned golden brown.

I still have the slightly tarnished teaspoon she used to measure the cookie dough full of Nestle's Toll House Semi-Sweet Chocolate Morsels that we lined up neatly on the two baking sheets discolored from age. Mom always added an extra handful of chocolate chips because "you can never have too much chocolate."

We are gathered around the clawfoot oak dining table exchanging anecdotes, the misty memories of a good childhood in a happy, safe home. The funeral was lovely. This was expected with Rabbi Friedman officiating. He had known Mom and Dad for thirty years and had now led us gently through that valley of death for the second time.

Sitting shiva, in Judaism, means gathering with friends and family for a week after a loved one is laid to rest. The food flows from the kitchens of others as ours stays idle. The mirrors in the home are covered and we wear a torn black ribbon over our heart as a symbol of the piece that cannot be mended.

Mother left each of her three children one special something. My piece of childhood is her file of recipes. She knew I loved to cook and we had exchanged recipes often over the last ten years. I turn the metal clasp that held the treasure trove of the past within the edges of the brown plaid tartan binder. My eyes race past the sheets of yellowing pages of shared tastes from her childhood and college friends. I gravitate to the last section labeled "Desserts" in my mother's perfect handwriting.

At the top was a morsel of family history. A recipe from Margaret, my grandfather's cook and friend and a letter to my mother. The handwriting was a little shaky, but showed hints of a young heart and a woman of experience.

Dear Gertrude,

I know you and your family love my chocolate cake each Thanksgiving, so I appreciate your asking for the recipe. I affectionately called it "My Deep Dark Chocolate Cloud". I have not made this in over 30 years so this task is daunting. I am piecing together the ingredients and recreating in my mind the steps and the details of how I did it. It was as if providence guided my hands with my dear mother looking over my shoulder.

As you can see, I'm from the old school and never wrote anything down. I use my guts as much as my mind. If I thought something was not right, I would add a little more. I never really measured anything. I used my judgement and it usually seemed to turn out okay. I hope you can understand what I have written and can use your common sense when you make it. As I recall you took directions well when you were young and seemed to catch on quickly.

Let me know how you make out.

I do very little baking or cooking these days. My hands are not as strong and they shake some, so I can't knead bread quite as well as I used to. For years baking was good therapy and strengthened my hands, until the arthritis set in. Sadly, now I just get it from the store.

I hope your family has a wonderful Christmas and Hannukah

If there is anything you need to know when you make the cake just give me a call.

All my love,

Margaret

    I stop reading this piece of history and close my eyes. My fingers rub the throbbing place on my forehead. I imagine I am back with Margaret in her kitchen with the open shelves full of canned preserves warmed by her oven at its center. I remember playing at my mother's feet as they cooked together.

***

Margaret Johnson places the pen down softly on the worn desk in the corner of her kitchen where she has spent most of her last days. She feels the warm sun as it touches her weathered brown skin through the lace curtains billowing in from the south facing windows. She smiles as thoughts race past of hard times that are finally being erased by the wonderful years with family and friends. It has been a good, long life and much that she remembers took place in this room. It seems like yesterday, but she knows that her aging mind is playing tricks. Her daughter, nicknamed Sissy, spent most Saturdays standing with her, absorbing life lessons like a human sponge. As a child, she used to drag the wooden step stool from under the island so she could easily reach the counter where Margaret conjured her magic. She outgrew the stool, but never the need to be by her side.

They recreated all the hand-me-down recipes of the Johnson home. Chicken and velvety smooth dumplings were a staple. This was served with butter beans and okra that were steaming as they made it to the table. On Sundays, the sizzling sound of Nana's Hand-Me-Down Fried Chicken and fried green tomatoes buzzed throughout the house. Crispy outside and juicy from the first bite. There was always dessert. Bubba's Banana Pudding with the vanilla wafer crust, or the Deep Dark Chocolate Cloud Cake. These recipes were guarded by the generations of Johnson family cooks who passed them along to sons, daughters and grandchildren.

Margaret blinks away the tears starting to form in the corners of her eyes. She does not remember a great deal now, but she can still recall the feel and smell of the food. Now she is the last person who retains any of this first-hand. Sissy passed two years ago and with her went most of the recipes committed to memory. Others in the family knew of Margaret and the love that she had sown. She encouraged and taught by example. But the world was too busy and moved too fast so the younger generation did not have an appreciation of the haunting passage of time and how it affected the center of the home, the kitchen.

    She places the letter to Miss Gertrude in the envelope, affixes a stamp and adds it to the corrugated box on the island along with the others. Her grandson, Jacob, will take them down to the post office at the back of Grayson's General Store tomorrow. She looks with satisfaction at the many letters she has finally completed to try and pass on the little bit of heritage she still possesses. With a weary sigh, she labors up the wooden stairs to her bedroom for a nap even though it was not time. Leaning back on the down pillow, she closes her eyes and dreams the same dream that makes her smile as she floats weightless above the gable roofs of this old Victorian home.

***

    I fold the letter and the recipe and place it back in the file. I gather these memories and pass over my parents' threshold for the last time. My plan? Take The Recipe home and attempt to duplicate the "Deep Dark Chocolate Cloud" tomorrow with my children at my side.

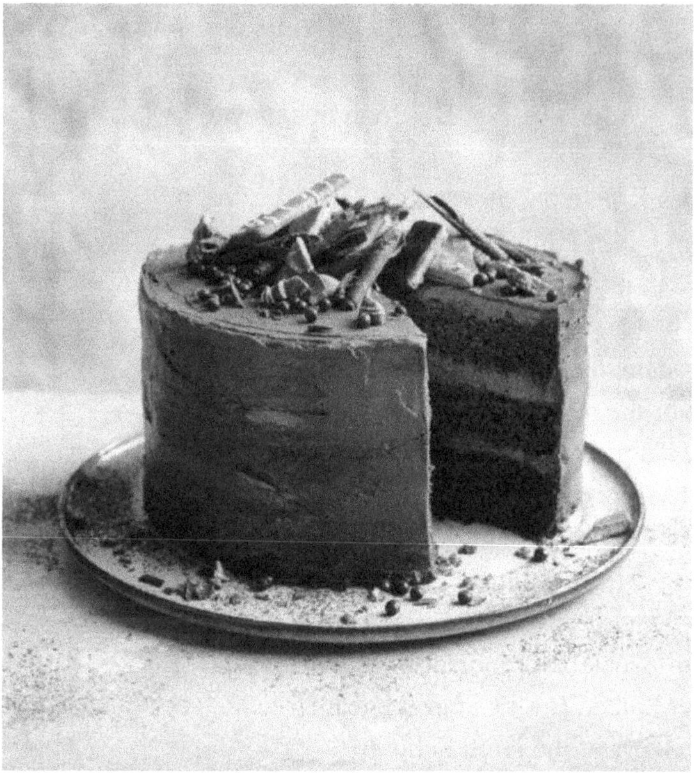

Cold Sweat

By: John Stickney

James Brown had it wrong.
1977 Junior High Sock Hop
Held in my 7th Grade Gym
My hand was anything but
Fast dancing with Carol Davis
She of the reddish brunette hair
The tan panty hose and short
Tight skirt.
My sisters Hully Gullyed me,
Shing-a-Ling-Ed me and showed
Me the virtues of the Mashed Potato
A full week before, drilled by two
Fleet Footed Boot Camp Sergeants
Survivors of the High School
Line Dance wars. I was battle ready.
But when a slow dance came,
The chance to hold her hand
To place my hand on her waist
And then her hip,
To hold each other close enough
That I could smell her cherry lip gloss
And she my beechnut gum,
My hand became a trickle,
And then a stream
As did hers
Not at all a cold sweat
And when the next 45
Popped into 'Papa's Gotta Brand New Bag'
She said, she loved the way

My feet moved
As I camel walked my way
Into a cold sweat.

Still Feel All of That Love From Here

By: Lorraine Gilmore

I had to leave. Mama understood that. She said I had to try my wings and fly. Mama understood because she wanted to do the same thing. Her family never had a lot of money. Her Pa had worked all his life on their farm. Mama was the youngest of eight. Her chores on the farm were always light with so many older kids to help with the work. She met my Daddy when they were in high school.

Mama was smart and did well in school. She would have gone on to college, but she met Daddy and got pregnant. College became just a dream. Daddy also grew up on a farm. As a young boy he took care of the chickens. He was the oldest of six and the farm came to him when his Pa died. It was a good thing because none of his brothers and sisters wanted to continue doing farm work.

All of us kids grew up with farm chores, but Mama made sure that we studied hard. She wanted her dream to live on through us.

But I was the only one that liked school. The other five were content with the life on the farm. All of us were lucky that we grew up in a house filled with love. You could feel Mama and Daddy's love because of the way they looked at each other. I never heard either of them raise their voice in anger even though they had plenty of arguments. They never had to raise their voices to us either. All it took was the stink eye and the use of our full name.

It was a good thing that I finished top of my class because I was offered a full scholarship to several good colleges. Mama and Daddy only had to scrape together the money for my books.

So here I am at Boston University and I'm ready to try those wings. It's a little scary to be so far from home. And, the people talk funny. Of course, they think I'm the one that talks funny. I seem to be the only one in my classes from the South. I miss the farm. The air was always clean and fresh. I guess it was 'cause we lived out in the country away from the sounds and smells of a busy city. It's so different here. Lots more cars and people and they're always moving. There were always a lot of chores on the farm, but we had time to sit under a tree and day dream. It seems these people always need to be busy. And, they talk fast. Sometimes I feel like I've traveled to a foreign country because it's so different.

Life seemed more simple back on the farm. I miss being there. I miss helping Mama with some of the house chores. On wash day, we would take the clean clothes and hang them on the lines in the backyard. I can still see the sheets waving in the wind and the smell of them after they dried in the sunshine and fresh air.

Most of all I miss the family dinners and the smells from the kitchen. Mama would make fresh rolls. There's nothing like the smell of baking bread as it spreads to the dinner table. Mama was a good cook. We ate a lot of chicken because the chicken coop was always full. Most days I was the one to walk among them sprinkling corn on the ground for them to eat and then collect the eggs they had laid. I named a few of the egg layers because so few of them ever had their necks rung. Mama was good at that when she needed one to cut up for supper. One of my favorite meals was chicken and dumplings. Mama made her own dough, rolled it out and cut it into strips which were placed in the hot broth. They were so tasty and full of flavor.

I think I'll write Mama a long letter. There's so much to tell her about Boston. I'll tell her how much I miss being

home on the farm.
    She'll be able to feel all of my love from there.

    Writing Prompt: All of That Love From Here as sung by Wynonna Judd

Love is Love

By: Terry L. Dismore

If you love, then love already
Life is too short for complicated
roses are red violets are blue
mushy you complete me stuff

If you care, then care
If you love then love

Hug, kiss, smile, embrace
and show tender love

Stop thinking
and love already

Limerick in Blue I

By: Claudia Blanchard

There once was a cop named Chauvin
Who really knew how to kill 'em
No peace officer he
When down on one knee
Would press the breath right out of him

Limerick in Blue II

By: Claudia Blanchard

There once was a boy Daunte Wright
Got stopped by the cops at a light
Got scared, started to run
Got shot by a gun
One more black body *yahrzeit**

**Hebrew – anniversary of a death memorialized by the burning of a candle.*

Plugging into the Future

By: Diane Pascoe

"Hey Di," my husband Eric exclaimed. "I just made appointments for us to try out one of those Tesla electric cars and the VW electric car too."

"Eric, we don't need a new car," I stated firmly. "Mine works fine and so does yours." Knowing he is an early adapter of all new technology, I was highly skeptical that he was just car window shopping. He was actually new car hunting, but he first needed to test drive some cars. I have learned a lot about him in our thirty-four years together so I can't be fooled.

Our neighbor, Mike, had also booked a test drive and his wife, Donna, was going along for the ride. There was no danger of Mike or Donna wanting a new car as they had recently bought a new Volvo and a BMW, so they were all set.

"Donna is going to test drive a Tesla with Mike," Honey stated. "If you go with me, then you can talk cars with her afterwards."

Yeah, right, Honey. Donna and I will talk recipes, decorating, and shoes. No car talk for sure.

But I figured that a lunch out, and maybe even an ice cream cone, might follow the test drives. It's all about the food with me, so I agreed to go.

We arrived at Mayfair Town Center where two Tesla cars were parked on the patio in front of the movie theatre—a sedan and an SUV. This was not a dealership.

Kevin, a young salesperson from Tesla, came over to educate us about their electric cars. Kevin was not a car guy really, he explained. He was an IT guy.

I quickly realized that this car is unlike any I have encountered. We were sitting in the front seats of a spaceship.

No dashboard. Almost no knobs or dials. Just a 17-inch screen with all the car statistics, maps, music, and guides that a human being would need. Kevin explained the functions of the screen including the ability to watch Netflix when the car is stopped. He also showed us how we could listen to Elton John or the Beatles on our drive. He had our ages nailed correctly.

Kevin explained about Tesla's quick turbo-charging stations as well as how to charge the car at home and at other places along the route to any destination, all displayed on that 17-inch screen. "Range anxiety" is the biggest barrier for people considering buying an electric car, Kevin said.

After 15 minutes of explanation, Kevin sent us off for a test drive in this Model Y spaceship. Smooth, quiet, sleek, with that big screen guiding us as we drove around town. Unbelievable. Eric offered me the driver's seat. No way—I would need a week of lessons to feel comfortable.

After discussing the car with Kevin, Eric asked for Kevin's business card. *No Eric,* I thought to myself, *this kid isn't a business-card guy*. Sure enough, true to Tesla's values, Kevin asked, "Eric, can I add my name to your contacts? Tesla tries to respect the environment."

The conversation turned to the process for buying a Tesla. "You can order online," Kevin said. "There is no dealer parking lot."

We have just moved into the future. Very weird.

We drove home talking non-stop about our out-of-body experiences with this machine, loosely called a car. Eric was soon back online learning more about this futuristic vehicle.

"Do you like the red or white exterior?" he asked, not so innocently.

Oh no—it's the alternate-choice sales closing focusing on color which is the only car feature I truly care about.

Honey is in his sales mode to sell me, his wife, on our need to get a Tesla for our family.

"But you want me to be happy, don't you?" he implored when I called him out on his Tesla sales tactics.

"No, I want <u>me</u> to be happy! Making you happy costs a lot of money—I can be happy for much less!"

Later, we also test drove the VW electric car. Much more car–like, but still smooth and quiet like the Tesla Model Y. A smaller interactive screen, but like the Tesla, the screen talked to us. I liked that.

"Isn't it cool?" said Honey.

I had to admit he was right.

The future is here I realized, so we need to get ready to plug into it. I don't know exactly when or which brand or which model we will buy, but it will happen much sooner than later.

There is no turning back.

Aunt Edith

By: Lorraine Gilmore

It's summer on Cape Cod and I have come to South Yarmouth for my two-week vacation. It's good to get away from the city and smell the breeze off the ocean as I wiggle my toes in the sand and take a sip of Molson which I have disguised with a Pepsi wrapper. This is a must as no alcohol is allowed on the beach.

South Yarmouth, MA is a typical town on Cape Cod. It is mid-Cape with Barnstable and Hyannis to the West and Dennis to the East. There are a few roads in this town with quaint names – Uncle Ephraim's Way, Aunt Dora's Road, and Syritha's Way which was my address for a few years. Then there is Aunt Edith's Road. That's the name of the street on which my Aunt Edith and her husband lived. Some coincidence, huh?

I used to spend a week with my Aunt Edith and Uncle Henry when I was in grade school. She's been dead for about twenty years. As I sit and watch the surf roll in, I still remember the good times we had.

She and Uncle Henry bought their house about thirty years ago. They had been looking for a home on the Cape when the realtor gave them a call about that one. Not only was it affordable, but they liked it before ever going inside because the back of the property faced a marsh. They knew that this would give them privacy and there might be some wildlife attracted to the marsh. Another key element was the boardwalk through the marsh which ended on a dock on the Bass River. After they purchased the house, they bought a twenty-seven-foot boat with a double bunk, toilet and a small kitchen below deck.

Every weekend during that first summer on the Cape, they would take the Not A Finger out for an overnight trip. Aunt Edith and Uncle Henry loved those trips. She would make them simple meals which they could eat in the cabin or up on the deck. She told me that they would start with drinks and a snack. They found it very relaxing to sit and watch the sun set as the boat bobbed along on the anchor. After supper, they would enjoy an after-dinner drink as they watched the moon rise among the twinkling stars.

On one weekend, they took me along and since the weather was good, I slept in a sleeping bag up on deck. When I asked Aunt Edith about the name, she said that she picked it out because she wouldn't have to lift a finger to do housework when they were out on the boat.

Uncle Henry really loved going out on that boat. He was a busy real estate lawyer and it was the one place where he could totally get away from his high-pressure job and relax. It was unfortunate that only several years after they moved to the Cape that he died. It was sudden and unexpected. He was a Marine and was in Korea for two years when his unit came under heavy fire for several hours. He was severely injured by shrapnel. He got good care in the field and at Walter Reed, but some of the shrapnel could not be removed. His doctor said that a piece moved and caused the heart attack.

Aunt Edith was devastated. They had been happily married for thirty-seven years and he was her whole life. Because of severe endometriosis, she was unable to have children and they had never wanted to adopt.

Although it was hard on Aunt Edith, she didn't sit around and mope. Uncle Henry had called her his little firecracker, because she had such vitality and a lust for life. After he died and the estate was settled, she spent a year traveling and then settled back into her life on the Cape. She always had plenty of interests which kept her busy and even took up a few new ones. She bought herself a canoe and often loaded it onto her car so that she could explore other rivers on the Cape. As she got older, she switched to a small kayak because it was easier for her to lift it into the back of the SUV.

I was glad that I was able to spend a lot of time with her on the Not A Finger. I got to go on some of those overnight trips and sleep in Uncle Henry's bunk. Aunt Edith didn't have to lift a finger when I was around. I was happy to take care of her and let her relax.

Prompt: Aunt Edith's Road

Isn't Life Just Like That?

By: Suzy Tenenbaum

A friend's mother-in-law died last week.
Another friend called with the news of a new grandchild.

Isn't life just like that?

What is it they say-
When one door closes, another opens?

Not necessarily for you
At exactly the same moment.
But over time
It seems we take turns.

It's like being on the see-saw on the playground.
You and your friend
Up and down,
Sometimes bumping too hard hitting the ground,
Sometimes flying too high,
Or for a moment pausing to balance-
Both level off the ground,
Then up and down again.

Isn't life just like that?

And you think maybe next time
You'll stay on the swings,
With your head back, eyes to the sky.
Sometimes there's no one to push you
And the chains get tangled.

Isn't life just like that?

Yet what a ride-
Life!
Our own personal park of experiences,
No two the same,
Thrills and chills.
Joys and sorrows,
Your own mystery book,
With an unknown ending.

Isn't life just like that?

"Don't cry because it's over, smile because it happened."
- *Dr. Seuss*

Animals and Tools, Tools and Animals

By: John Stickney

It is a puzzle
These animals
And their sudden use
Of tools

The squirrel,
Wrench in paws,
Opening the top
Of the bird feeder

The rabbits,
Ear tips visible
Out of the back
Of their hardhats,
Jackhammering
The ground to reach
The root vegetables

And the birds
With their slings and arrows
Always patrolling
Awaiting the right moment

Of course,
not everything
Has been peaceful.

The ducks want
The can opener

For the creamed corn
And the dogs
The same for the bounty
Of canned dog food.

Cats, it must be noted,
Can't be bothered
With this new and
Oh so boring, technology.

Rats and other vermin
Bide their time
Secure knowing
There's always enough
Waste and garbage
No matter who's
In charge.

The Repo Man Sucks Wind

By: Lee Norman Meheler

"Put my vacuum down. You can't take it. I only owe three hundred more."

I stared at the mousey little woman tightly gripping her Hoover and laughed. Her skin stretched tightly on her slight, hunched-over frame. I guess my soul had hardened since the first time I did a collection three years ago. Mrs. Creech looked like a paler version of my grandmother. but I just didn't give a shit.

"Not my problem, Enid. I warned you last month. There was a grace period in March, but your time is up. Big Eddie says it's the money or the goods. That vacuum is mine now. And don't forget all the attachments."

"But I have made four payments of three hundred dollars each for this sucker, and I almost got caught up. Only one left," she whimpered.

"I know you took on extra cleaning shifts to pay for this essential tool of your trade." Enid thought she could clean up with this extra fancy five speed vacuum with infrared sensors and double strength edge cleaning. "But I warned you. Buying a Cadillac for your new janitorial service when a basic Chevy would do the same job was not the smartest move."

The lights in the living room seemed to dim. The air stopped moving. There was a tinge of mold…or something recently dead all around.

Enid's eyes changed. They got grayer and darker. Her features hardened and her mouth started chanting something silently. She took a step forward…then another. She looked through me and I shuddered. There was nothing left behind her cold, vacant stare.

She slowly raised her hands above her head.

"What is that, Enid?" I could not make out what she held aloft with the glaring bathroom light behind her.

"You have left me no choice. This is my implement of last resort!"

She let the feather duster come down over my head with a swoosh of cold air. I cringed and screamed at the same time. It tickled and made me laugh so hard that my heart skipped a beat...and then another. The pollen and the dust mites flowed into every pore and up my nose. I could not breathe! My throat tightened. I clawed at the air. I lunged at Enid in a desperate try to stop her attack and silence her addled laughter. I was experiencing that dreaded thing that I had read at the climax of my favorite mystery books.

My life flashed before my eyes in slow motion, and I had nothing but regret.

The gang at the bar would never stop having fun at my expense when they got the report from Detective Stone the next day. I was found lying in the alley behind the house. My body was contorted and swollen from a massive case of hives. My eyes were bulging out of my sockets. I had lost control of any remaining dignity. My epi-pen was only a foot from my grasp when I took my last breath.

Big Eddie would have to wait for that final payment, and I would not be making the collection.

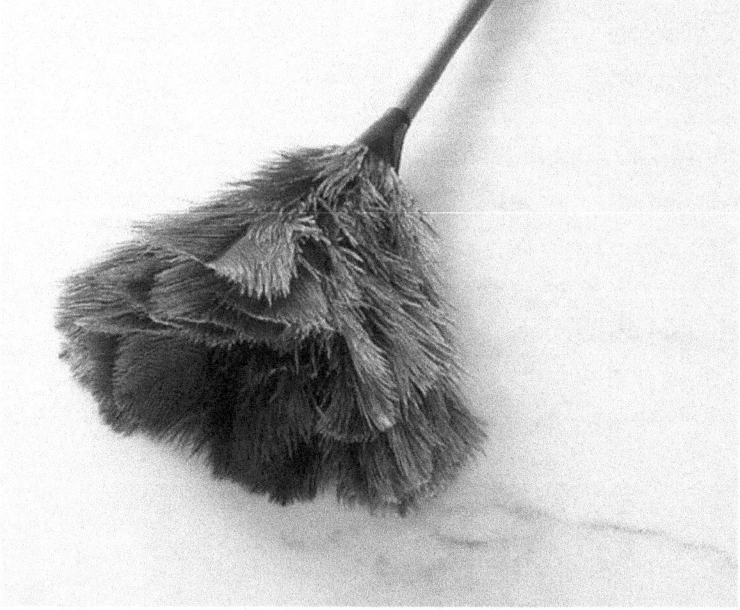

It Started to Rain

By: Terry L. Dismore

Rain rain go away
come again another day

Little drops little drops
now a drizzle
too late to stop

Can't stand-by and ignore
the drowning cries
for our **country to survive**

Torrential differences
stop them at the drop!

Josie

By: Barbara Dullaghan

The first time I met Josie, I felt drawn to her deep brown eyes and billowing black curly hair that seemed to have a life of its own. Her sense of humor and devious laugh endeared me as she recounted her many attempts to find a roommate who wasn't psychotic or didn't sleep with a knife under her pillow.

I could relate to that, not the knife, but the psycho part. I asked one potential roomie if she had pets. She told me she had a pet frog which she let out of his cage when she was home from work to roam around. Sometimes he even slept on the pillow next to her face.

"Let's just say she didn't make the cut," I told Josie. We shared a chuckle about that one.

After an hour of chatting, I thought I had a good idea about her when we agreed to be roommates. None of her answers had alarmed me. So, I confided in her that I was incredibly freaked out by clowns.

"Clowns freak ME out too!" she gushed.

Her eyes grew really large and she avoided my gaze which creeped me out. But when she giggled that little laugh, the hairs on the back of my neck stood up. I brushed it off thinking it must be my imagination.

Josie moved in when I was at work. I returned to the apartment looking forward to enjoying a glass of red wine after a particularly hectic day at the office, solving everyone else's problems.

But what did I find?

Giant balloons of clown faces bumped into my face as I walked into the living room. Disoriented, I almost tripped over the three huge frogs jumping around my feet, one clinging to my leg like it was a tree trunk. I screamed as I swatted the slimy thing away.

The sound of metal scraping drew my eyes to the corner of the room. There sat Josie in my comfy chair, raising a glass of red wine to me in one hand while wielding a knife in the other.

"Welcome home, Roomie!"

Deleted

By: John Stickney

Working from today's prompt… Somehow I deleted Lorraine's email*

Somehow I deleted Lorraine's email. I claim full responsibility, except it really wasn't my fault. And besides what exactly is email? A series of dots and dashes, of wave and particle, of white white light and electrical impulses, a blink in another world. One could argue that an email is so ephemeral it does not really exist.

Somehow I deleted the Magna Carta. Unfortunately, due to historical precedent we now are back in a feudal society. Your wares and goods are subject to the Crown. Your first-born male is a mandated soldier, your second a monk, your third must till the Royal lands. Your daughters may serve, may cook, may warm a bed. For my children's sake I hope I can find the button that will un-delete the deleted Magna Carte.

Somehow I deleted the human part of humanity. Most folks won't notice, they were less human a long time ago. Soon Chimeras** will be the norm.

Somehow I forgot to delete from my history that website that should've been deleted.

Somehow I forgot to delete my life-like hairpiece, with matching life-like mustache. Neither had much life in them. The ad promised:

DON'T BE AN OBJECT OF RIDICULE
LOOK AS YOUNG AS YOU ARE WITH A LIFE LIKE HAIRPIECE
CALL MODERN BARBERS PHONE 777 - 6650.

And in small print Halloween rentals, which should've been the tip off. Somehow I forgot to delete that ad before acting on it.

Somehow I forgot to delete my body's timetable. Old age stuff is annoying and wearying. At night the lamp questions my ability to sleep. My memory is not what it used to be. Did I mention that at night the lamp questions my ability to sleep?

Somehow I forgot to delete my pretend letter of credit. Well, according to the indictment, not pretend but what does a random collection of twelve strangers really know?

Somehow I forgot to delete the knife in my sock, the broken antenna which could be used like a whip tucked in my right pant leg, the five shot S&W revolver strapped to my ankle (the other ankle not the one with the knife), and the taser hidden in my cell phone holder. I forgot to delete these before trying to board the airplane. Assured by the TSA they'd be kept for safekeeping, like any real American, I was allowed to climb aboard. By the way, they missed the brass knuckles and the box cutter.

I should've deleted the idea of writing this piece. Sometimes when you're pressed for time you just make questionable decisions. It's part of being - I'd like to say human - more likely it's part of being part monkey, part man, and whatever else they forgot to delete from that test tube.

In our weekly WOTF writing practice, we are given prompts to inspire us to write something, anything, for twenty minutes and then share the results. During most of 2019 and 2020, our meetings were via Zoom, our prompts sent via email. One week the email about prompts began: "I accidentally deleted Lorraine's email." I chose to use that as my prompt.

**A chimera is essentially a single organism that's made up of cells from two or more "individuals"—that is, it contains two sets of DNA, with the code to make two separate organisms.

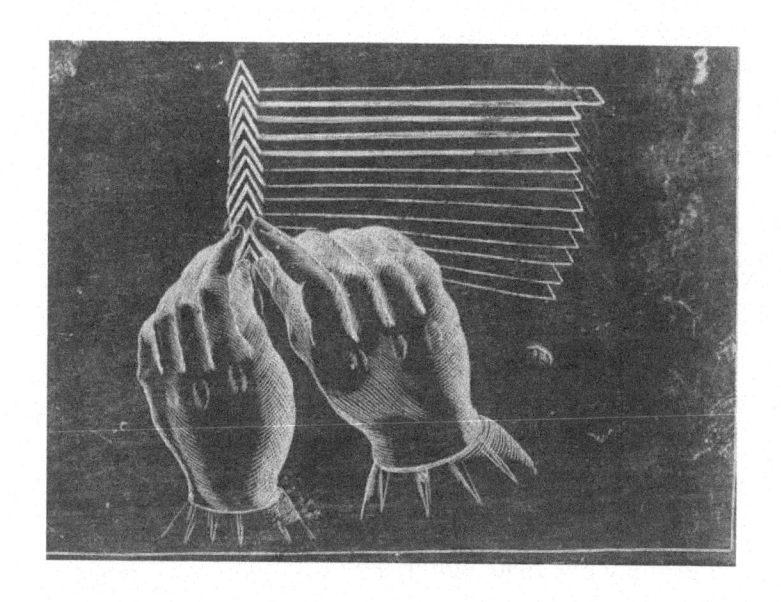

Cupboard Conversations

By: Suzy Tenenbaum

The white glass pan used for Luke's lasagne
calls to me from the cupboard.
I wave at it, back there tucked away.

What is it about dishes?
They insist on being acknowledged,
calling out, "Remember me?"

That flowered teacup gives a queen's wave,
reminding me of mornings with my mom and
how she encircled it with her spotted hand.

The blue and white plate which held
the brownies baked by my long-gone sister,
gives me a nod, as I lower it from the cabinet.

"Hey, it's been a while," calls out the party platter
"Come on, make some appetizers;
I could use some fun!"

Tonight I don't have time for these conversations,
so it's take out from the nearby restaurant,
and dinner is served on paper plates.

The Real Story of Cinderella

By: Lorraine Gilmore

Some people do not know how to tell a story because they always want to embellish and prettify what really happened. It's my story to tell and I think you will agree that it's still a good story when I stick to the facts.

First of all, let's start with my name. My parents never called me Cinderella. I was their only child and they named me Beatrice, which means she who makes happy. They waited many years for a child. They were lovely people who died in a tragic accident when a rabbit spooked their team of four and the carriage plunged over a cliff. I was an only child and it was up to my father's sister to take me in.

Aunt Agatha had plenty of money, but her heart was very tiny and this meant that all of her love was given to her two daughters, Hazel and Gwendolyn. She doted on them and gave in to their every desire. Hazel and Gwendolyn also had tiny hearts and did not want to share their mother with me. That part of the story which you have heard is true. I was dressed in their hand-me-down clothes and made to clean up after them and this included maintenance of the fireplace in their bedrooms. I had to bring in the wood, clean out the cinders and make sure that the room was warm and toasty at all times. They were the only ones to call me Cinderella.

And you can forget about the fairy godmother, the mice and the pumpkins. You can blame all of that folderol on Walt Disney.

I am a most resourceful young woman. I had to be in order to survive in that household. I planned well in advance how I would go to the palace ball. I taught myself to sew because I had to mend my clothes and theirs. Aunt Agatha was stingy with the hand-me-downs. The dressmaker never seemed to miss the fabric that I was able to purloin from her supplies. The gown which I made was not fancy, but it was quite flattering to my figure.

The ride to the palace: all of the hard work kept me agile and athletic. I was able to climb on the back of the coach as it pulled away from the front door. It meant hanging on for dear life, but I managed. Hazel and Gwendolyn were too busy with their own chatter and the coachmen were pre-occupied with their duties to notice me swinging in the wind.

It took some doing, but I made my way to the ballroom by going in the back entrance. I slipped into the kitchen and followed one of the servants taking champagne up to the ballroom. I was careful and quiet and again no one paid any attention to me.

I think it was my hair that caught the attention of the prince. I had taken two red roses from Aunt Agatha's prize rose bush and pinned them in among my curls. He bowed low over my hand and asked me for a dance. The prince was not only charming, he had gorgeous brown eyes and a warm smile. I loved the feeling of floating around the dance floor as he held me close in his arms.

We didn't need a lot of words between us, but I felt that each of us knew that we had a strong attraction to each other. We danced every dance together until it got quite late. I knew I could not stay until the very end of the ball and would have to leave early so that I could be at the door to greet Aunt Agatha and her daughters when they arrived home. She would expect me to take their cloaks and hang them up. As the clock began to strike mid-night, I curtsied to the prince and ran from the ballroom. In my haste, one of my slippers fell from my foot onto the stairs going out of the palace.

Lucky for me, a neighbor's carriage was just leaving and I was able to hang off the back of it.

Imagine my surprise when the family came home and were talking about the mysterious dance partner of the prince. They had not recognized me dressed in my beautiful gown.

Several days later the prince and several members of his court arrived at the house. The head footman carried my slipper on a cushion and said they were looking for the young girl who had danced with the prince. I knew it was my slipper because I had sewn several roses onto each of them.

There was no chance that the big footed step-sisters would fit into my small slipper no matter how hard they tried. As they were leaving the house, the footman noticed me standing to one side. I was holding the matching slipper in my hand and I winked at him as he looked from the slipper to my face.

I forgave Aunt Agatha and her daughters. The prince was willing to let them live in a very comfortable suite in the East Wing of the palace. We never see them, but they are more comfortable than they were in their small house.

The prince and I are living in the West Wing.

You've probably heard the correct ending to my story. We are very happy together and have two lovely children.

Sunrise Sunset

By: Terry L. Dismore

Sunrise Sunset
What an honor to
watch another
sunrise sunset

If you're reading this poem,
you've beaten the odds for living
and watching
another sunrise
another sunset

Witness as often as you can

'Twas Beauty Killed the Beast

By: Claudia Blanchard

It was fentanyl in his system
It was methamphetamine
It was an enlarged heart
It was a narrowing of the coronary arteries
It was asphyxia
It was cardiopulmonary arrest
It was carbon monoxide poisoning

No!

It was Derek Chauvin who murdered George Floyd.

What We Threw At The Monster

By: John Stickney

As we frolicked in the night woods, in what we imagined as Gypsy style, a pot of communal stew suspended over a fire, straw covered bottles of homemade wine and spirts, one dangling earring each, hair bandana wrapped, music made for slightly twirling, the Monster entered the fire lit clearing from the woods.

Gus, who was not a Gypsy, heck, none of us were, threw first his bow and then his violin. The Monster caught one, then the other, tipped an imaginary cap and shuffled off, back out of the light and up the mountain.

The next day, after we broke camp and began our trek home, the woods filled with the mournful sound of a cartoon cat perched on a cartoon fence, calling for a mate in the night. And we, in our cartoon beds of our cartoon houses, contemplated throwing a shoe out the window. Tempting. But we needed both our shoes to leave.

Over the next few times in the woods we threw: a good luck pebble, a thumb (one of our numbers worked in the County Coroner's office, stating, 'Trust me, that guy had way bigger issues than a missing thumb"), a bit of pitch, a self-winding clock, a tome entitled "On The Metaphysics of Silence", the video tape of "How to Play the Violin Like Stephane Grappelli", a portable battery operated VHS player, one black swan, some Skoal chewing tobacco, a mail man's uniform, that mother of pearl harmonica you can hear right now playing 'Lazybones', influenza, fear of inflation, all our unused melancholy…some other things.

Now, older, we are less given to walking sticks, more walking canes. We rarely visit, rarely still frolic, no longer throw. The Monster must make do, like us, on what it managed to squirrel away for these wet, rainy remaining days.

Fragile

By: Suzy Tenenbaum

That egg is fragile, hold it carefully
Mama told me
And I did, well I tried my best
But it slipped when I was opening the latch

Mama said nothing

I looked down and saw the yellow on my shoe
I stopped
Stood still
Tears streamed down my face
Mama pulled a tissue out of her pocket
And wiped my cheek

We'll get eggs again tomorrow
Mama said
I nodded and slipped my hand into hers
I thought she'd tell Daddy
When we went back in the house

Mama said nothing

Finality

By: Lorraine Gilmore

I don't know what tomorrow will bring.
Dark clouds overwhelm my soul.
My heart is frozen with anger.

Events have brought me to my knees.
I lie here immobilized by my grief.
My sorrow fills all my being.

The night seems endless
as I wait for sleep.

Hours pass and
my eyes finally close.
The dreams of you begin.

We are young again and
greedy for the delight brought
by physical intimacy.
The joy brings tears to my eyes
Which sour as I become aware
That this dream will end and
I will awaken to another day
without you.

Sorrow overwhelms me and
fills all my being.
I know it will end only
when I join you in death.

Inspiration: the two phrases came to me –
I don't know what tomorrow will bring
and
Sorrow fills all of my being

In Honor of Women's History Month

By: Terry L. Dismore

Women possess the fertilized
enriched soil cultivating
the universal life force for us all

Women **toil in the soil**
never ending river
multiplying seeds for the world's surrender

Standing on the shoulders of
**Harriet, Ruth, Theresa, Sacajawea,
Ester, and many others**

Women gird your loins in plated armor
claiming **peace** and **protection**
against hatred, violence ravaging our land

Proclaimed Mothers of the Earth
take your unseen seeing eye
ready to protect past
present and future

**We exist because you exist
Without you there is no me
I am you and You are Me**

Primal drums feverishly beating
signaling, continuing
weaving DNA

The universal Mother God forecast
a downpour of afternoon showers
commanding the removal
of girded armor
calling
future She-roes
ready to be born

Amanda
Kamala
Michele
Nancy
Granddaughter Charlie
ready to take your place

Anointed oil
nine months in the soil
nourished with love not hate

Dancing clouds
flickering promise of a
new world for you and me

The trees are greener
than ever before
wind sounds different
air smells fresh and clean

People smiling, loving, caring
for what the new day will bring
Listen to the whispers in the wind

Women
with full intention
recognition
proclamation

We exist because you exist
Without you there is no me
I am you and You are Me

When Day and Night is a Short Story

By: John Stickney

They say there
is no time

This place
is too small

Not everything
is quiet enough

Try to take
a breath
In that space
make a poem

The Keys of Life

By: Lee Norman Mehler

CAST OF CHARACTERS

NARRATOR:
The one who sets the stage, place and mood. He is dressed in gray and blends into the background when not speaking.

HORACE:
Horace West is 60 years old and dealing with the influence of his father. He is dressed casually in slacks, pale long-sleeved shirt with the sleeves rolled part of the way up and a vest. He has black rimmed glasses resting on his head. He has a three-day beard.

PERCIVAL WEST:
The gifted father and renowned jazz musician. His ability to communicate with a piano exceeds his ability to communicate with humans. He has a good heart but struggles to show it. He is dressed in light colored shirt and slacks, slightly unkempt. He is thin and tall, slicked back gray hair, clean shaven.

STACY:
Horace's wife of forty years is a former dancer who still keeps in shape. She wears loose, flowing dresses that allow her to move freely. Her long gray hair is kept up most of the time with a hair clip. She worries about Horace.

SETH:
The third brother of the talented West children, he has given up his link to the arts to become a businessman. He is the

practical one with short hair and reading glasses. He is quiet and introspective.

STAGING
The stage is black and bare. The overall space is lit in a pale half-light. Participants are on stools, separated. Lights are raised and lowered on each speaker as they speak.

PLACE AND TIME
The place and time floats with Horace's thoughts. He is caught between the here and now and the soon to be.

(Light jazz piano plays. C Jam Blues by Dave McKenna. Music fades as the dialog begins)

NARRATOR:
His name is Horace West. Percival West is his father.
The sacred monument stands against the wall in the spare bedroom. The upright Baldwin Hamilton piano sets off the wall eight inches so when Percival plays it reflects into the room and every corner of the house. Horace and the other children are allowed in the room only when their father grants his permission.

HORACE:
That room was supposed to be mine. I'm saying this for the record if anyone is listening.
The Baldwin Hamilton was the dominant icon in the room. The dark stained oak finish stood out against the light gray walls and the white bookcases full of sheet music, long playing albums and photo books. When you flipped up the wood keyboard cover it revealed a door to another world. My

father could transform those idle ivory and black keys into a magical sound ranging from the jarring discordant din of the subways below the street to the smooth silky sounds of the angels playing above.
My dad, Percival West, was a large man with a gentle touch. His big soft hands had long tapered fingers that could span eleven keys, more than any other piano player I ever knew. He had an ear for hearing things differently than most mortals. And his fingers moved as if each one had its own instinct. The notes that came off the Baldwin's soundboard was not of this world.

NARRATOR:
Stacy is Horace's wife of thirty years. She quietly lets Horace talk uninterrupted. She knows him well enough to sense when to be silent.

HORACE:
Do you know what it is like growing up with a father who has been declared a genius by everyone he touches?

NARRATOR:
Stacy sees the years etched in Horace's face. The skin wrinkles around his eyes as he squints, looking back to the past. His bushy mustache takes over as he bites his lower lip. She knows he will rewind his life and be mired in a bog of unjustified self-criticism. But he will come back to the present and his complicated reality if she just lets him talk. It is better to be doing this in their sunny living room surrounded by soft overstuffed cushions, rather than the hard seat of the local bar where he usually hangs out. Horace has not had a drink for a month. He just got his chip the day before at the meeting. Now he needs to review things again.

HORACE:
Dad wasn't a major asshole about his gift, just a minor one. He didn't know he was acting any different than the rest of us. He would spend hours hunched over that Baldwin composing and writing down melodies that came into his head at all hours of the day or night. He would leave the room without notice or saying a word, as if he were going to a fire. Sometimes in midsentence. Dad heard the world differently than others. He could absorb the sounds of life in the wind through the trees, the traffic on a summer day, or the high-pitched clatter of vendors on the street.
It's not that he didn't try in his awkward way. I remember him pulling me up on his knee when I was eight to explain the mechanics of a piano.

PERCIVAL WEST:
This is a complex instrument with eighty-eight keys and hammers striking strings and dampers and pedals. But none of that really means a damn. It's the soul of the man sitting in this seat coaxing the sounds to emerge that matters. You need to feel it in your every fiber, not just play. It's all dead unless you are alive.

HORACE:
We got used to the great Percival West's absence. Mom would continue the conversation without him, hardly missing a beat. Their communication was in a different language. Much like the jazz that dad was famous for. Everything was slightly askew, off kilter. They fought hard and lived hard. Verbally punched and counterpunched with ideas and concepts that we kids couldn't understand. As we grew up, he supported what we aspired to be, as long as it was in the arts. But he was

M.I.A. many times when we needed a parent. Mom tried to fill in, but with a brood of six she was spread thin.
Dad's music was mostly improvised as was his life. He wasn't really unfaithful to our mother or his children. Except he had a mistress named Jazz. If he wasn't slumped over the keyboard in the room down the hall, we knew he was at the Club Russo downtown.

NARRATOR:
The Club Russo was in the middle of the 200th block on Main Street. It was the last original storefront. Formerly a Speakeasy in the 20's, Max Pearson had saved it from the wrecking ball and bought it for ten cents on the dollar at auction. He restored the old brick and stucco shell to its original glory with music rolling out onto the street every night through open shutters that lured you inside.

HORACE:
On special occasions or holidays, we kids could sit at the back of the club for the first set. We could make out the ghost of our father in the corner of the stepped-up stage through the blue smoke. Sonny Jenkins was on the bass. He was skinny and seemed to curl himself around the instrument that was six inches taller than him. His sound rumbled under your seat and filled the dark corners of the room. Pete Cochrane was behind the drums and constantly in syncopated motion. He never missed a beat or a wordless cue from my father. I think he slept with those drumsticks. His hair was graying and his joints were aching. Josiah Peterson was the fourth wheel of the well-oiled machine they called the West Quartet. Josiah could play anything that required long wind and a soft touch. His trumpet reached highs and lows that were hard to comprehend. Josiah was round and sweaty after just the first few notes. But

Percival West was the glue that held this tight group together no matter where the melody led them on the stage or around the city.

NARRATOR:

Horace is silent for a moment. His face changes as the memories pass before his eyes in an instant. He is no longer smiling.

HORACE:

I couldn't play a note. Dad's body language expressed his disappointment. I developed my own fantasy world through acting and singing. I would escape the loneliness by being others. It frustrated my father that I had no interest singing jazz or blues. I found my home in Broadway show tunes. Dad spent the hours after midnight with his buddies Dave McKenna, or Charles Mingus, or Thelonious Monk, while I was in bed wanting to be Richard Burton, Robert Preston, Rex Harrison, or Gordon McRae.

I was the oldest and the first one to go to college. My gift to go on stage unafraid, consume a role and connect with an audience gave me a thrill even when I was young. I played with the idea of investing my soul into characters who were not me when I was in school. I approached my father and mother with the possibility of pursuing my love of theater before high school. We set a goal of earning enough to pay for a large chunk of my additional training. Mom worked overtime and I took on as many spare time jobs and summer gigs as I could. We knew Dad could not save much from his meager earnings as a musician but preserving his artistic drive was always deemed more important by the family.

NARRATOR:
Percival West was the hub of the family wheel. But he was a pragmatist when it came to bringing up a family. He knew he would depend on his wife to keep the six talented children completing their own agendas, even if they did not follow his.

HORACE:
I went to the state college with a decent acting school. I flourished under the wing of a professor who thought I had that undefined something to make it. But he was wrong. I was in the majority of people who don't make a living at what they love. I had minor successes at college and local productions that fed my need for expression and were an outlet for emotional connection. But all were fleeting and never added up to what my father had hoped for. I gravitated to the classics which is another way to not make a living in acting. Shakespeare and classic musicals are seldom paths to glory unless you live in an age of revivals. But I am who I am. You don't choose what or who you fall in love with all the time. Sometimes the love chooses you, unannounced.
And then, there's Stacy. We were in a local revival of Oklahoma as part of the supporting cast the summer of 1969. As Laurey and Curly performed their duets we were stage left doing our best to blend into the scenery and harmonize with the chorus. During the second act ensemble song "The Farmer and the Cowman" we were paired off and touched hands. There was something electric when we looked deeply into each other's eyes as directed by the choreographer. By the final reprise of "Oklahoma" our lives were linked beyond this stage. It was a mutual love by the second act. She has been my leading lady in search of an Act Three for all these years. She does her best to keep me focused whenever I want to improvise too much.

NARRATOR:

Stacy tries to let Horace take the lead.

STACY:

So, are you going to see him? Time is running out. Don't think about it too long, Horace.

HORACE:

I'm not sure what to do, or say.

NARRATOR:

Percival West has been slowed by a stroke. He has persevered through the many ailments that had threatened to pull him away from the piano. The arthritis has eaten away at his dexterity the last few years. But this minor stroke has caught him by surprise. Horace hears about it from his middle brother, Seth

SETH:

I think Dad has been hiding it for a while. You know how stubborn and private he can be. I'm not sure how long he has. Probably a good idea to come as soon as possible. Don't wait too long.

HORACE:

Stacy and I stop at the lower step of the front porch with the peeling white-wash paint. The pair of old rockers are still there but one seems smaller since mom passed. Dad has let the house go the last few years. There are terra cotta pots lining the porch with husks of plants beyond recognition.
What am I going to say, Stacy?

NARRATOR:
She did not answer right away, waiting a moment to allow the ghosts of this place to help find the words.

STACY:
Try to let go of your disagreements. They are not important now. There was a time when you two were more alike than different. Just speak from the heart. Let the last few years fade away and remember when you both were looking for your own answers, when the hurt didn't matter.

HORACE:
We go up the three steps, through the creaking screen door and push the heavy carved oak door open.
Stacy sits on the bench seat in the entrance hall with the high, echoing ceiling. A few lonely chords escape the room at the rear buffeted by the flow of the stale heated air. My head is full of stanzas of unwritten melodies.
I turn the corner and stop again when I see Dad leaning over the keys. His right hand lingers but his left hand moves easily to complete an ethereal phrase that would not come from his now silent lips. Time skips a beat but his music does not. The air is suddenly lighter and the sun streams in as it emerges from behind a cloud.

I know what to say.

(Music begins again by Dave McKenna. It increases in volume slightly then fades at Curtain.)

Dedicated to Doug McKenna and Dave McKenna who inspired the characters in this work of fiction.

Excerpts

Some Writers of the Forest are working on full length novels. The following section contains excerpts from those works.

The Relentless Anchor

By: John C. Stipa

Story synopsis:
Walt Unitus is a decent man trying to navigate the turbulent waters of life. He is plagued by bullies, learning disabilities and depression. But he forges ahead, determined to take care of his family, despite the relentless despair that drags him to unbearable depths, so deep that he contemplates suicide. His family comes to his aid and a fierce battle begins. Will Walt's demons overwhelm him, or can a family's love make a difference?

Chapter 1

It's come to this, Walt Unitus thought. The summation of a man's existence, all boiled down into one life altering decision.

No more pain. No more angst or humiliation. The time to be free. Free of worry. Free from doubt. Free to escape.

He set his chair down in an unclaimed patch of meadow next to a growth of honeysuckle. He swigged one last sip from his coffee cup, kicked off his hiking shoes and settled down, massaging the grass with his bare feet while inhaling a lung full of sweet flora.

Eyes gazing skyward, he sighed. A squadron of geese sailed into view, silent, their wings never moving, the glide holding them in perfect formation until they disappeared over the crest of Mount Astraea. A gentle rain speckled his face.

"Astraea," Walt mused. "How appropriate."

They called the place where the two rivers met "The Divining Rod". It gained its name by virtue of the "Y" formed by the merger of the Kwila river, the Lenape Indian word for death, and the Nulawsi, which meant life. At the crotch of the "Y" stood Mount Astraea, a narrow, two-faced mountain that resembled the head of an axe. The sharp point created the illusion it divided the rivers in two, when in fact they combined to form the river Kwishimao, the Lenape word for choice.

Did the Lenape really choose? Or was it fate?

Standing, Walt dumped his car keys and his coffee cup into the seat. He grabbed his hiking shoes and strolled to the edge of the Nulawsi river. Raindrops dappled the stream surface, disrupting the reflection of the mountain on the water.

Hmm, could Mr. Tremblay have been right?

Gingerly, Walt stepped down into the cool babble. The silt oozed softly on his feet and between his toes. A few strides delivered him to the opposite bank where a path of steps, carved by settlers from another era, provided the only way to scale the mountain to access the diving ledges that protruded from each face.

Is this how I want to be remembered?

The ledge above Nulawsi, while higher, proved safer than its brother due to the straight shot to the green pool below. Kwila, although lower, required a difficult leap outward to clear the stones to reach deep water.

It's only difficult if you try.

Slipping into his hiking shoes, Walt began the climb. The first few steps were easy and he took them two at a time. It reminded him of the trip to Italy when he and his daughter had scaled the Spanish Steps in Rome. Just as he had then, he tired now and slowed his ascent. Every few feet came a landing where he stopped to rest – and think.

How did I get to this point?

A multitude of memories invaded his thoughts. Recollections that highlighted both the good and the bad moments of his life. Winning his first game as a high school baseball pitcher, and then not making the team in college. His wedding day, and his wife's untimely death. The thrill of becoming a father, and the soul-sucking gut punch of his daughter's accident. The kind of memories that might flash through a person's mind in their last moments.

The honk of geese overhead returned Walt to the present. He resumed his climb until there were no more landings and no more steps. Only a drooping tree branch impeded his progress. Sweeping it aside, he froze as his breathing stuck in his chest. Beyond lay the spot where the path forked. To the left, Nulawsi and safety; to the right, Kwila and peril.

"Yes," he whispered, "it's all come down to this."

Where did it all go wrong?

A thousand rationalizations ran through his mind in the search for an answer. Eventually, he came back to the beginning, when his mother and father grappled with their financial struggles...

Guilt Will Lead the Way: A Bronze Lady Mystery (Unpublished)

By: Barbara Dullaghan

Story synopsis:
Carrie Peters is a forty-year-old woman, riddled with guilt and secrets, struggling to understand how she and her ex-boyfriend could have gotten things so wrong. Carrie's life is complicated when she returns to her hometown of Sleepy Hollow after her parents die. She still feels tremendous guilt for the suicide of her high school friend, a result of one of her indiscretions. Even though he's been dead for over twenty years, the memory continues to torment her. Carrie steals another friend's journal and discovers his knowledge of that grievous secret. Her best friend, a homicide detective, grows increasingly concerned about her erratic behavior.

Carrie has no one to turn to except her ex-boyfriend because he shares her secrets. But she finds it too painful to connect with him. He is a constant reminder of the life she lived and tried to leave behind. Carrie needs to deal with her guilt, but to do so she may have to confess her part in a life-changing incident and possibly risk her freedom.

Part One

Time often seemed to stop in the cemetery. The spring flowers were budding all around and the trees in full bloom. The sun had just set and the moon had not yet fully risen in the sky. This evening, a young boy's bloody body lay at the feet of the Bronze Lady. Just a few minutes before he had been his usual self: a bully, obnoxious and taunting. Now, with his brother kneeling over him, he was drifting in and out of consciousness and quietly bleeding. He could hear someone whimper and call his name. He could smell the earth on which he lay and, for a brief moment when his eyes fluttered open, he could see the Bronze Lady and a glimpse of his brother before all went dark.

Chapter 1

It stopped me in my tracks. Literally. My tracks in the crusty snow. The realization after twenty years that my mother was right; she didn't even know that I had secrets.

She'd say, "You can run but you cannot hide, Carolyn."

A list of my secrets would seem ridiculously endless, as if everything in my life was frightening. But it seemed that way to me.

Once, in an uncharacteristically weak moment, Mother admitted to me how sad she felt that I hadn't married and borne children, as if I couldn't have them without being married. Almost gave myself away then.

I am always running from something.

My feet were getting cold so I headed back to my house. Although it was early March, Plattsburgh's location ten miles from the Canadian border still meant snow on the ground.

Would I ever tell my mother that she had been right? For God's sake. Forty years old and I'm still worried about telling her everything? As I finished my run and rounded the corner by my house, my thoughts about my mother were suddenly interrupted. I noticed a police car and two officers standing outside my front door.

I stopped abruptly. *Is this happening? Now?* I slowly walked toward them. "Can I help you, officers?"

A burly cop with a dark black mustache turned to face me. "We are looking for Carolyn Peters. Is that you?"

"Yes, what's wrong? What happened?"

"I am Officer Cardell and this is Officer Simon. We're with the Plattsburgh Police Department," he said, as they flashed their badges. "May we talk with you inside?"

"Why?" I said as I fumbled with the keys to unlock the door.

"Are you the daughter of Philip and Marjorie Peters of Sleepy Hollow, New York?"

"Yes, please tell me what is going on."

The next twenty minutes were a blur of alarming and frightening images of a deadly crash with another car, presumably someone running a stop sign and plowing almost head on into my parents. As if to comfort me, the officer assured me they died together almost instantly.

This is unbelievable. Such a shock but it could have been worse. Right? Oh, God, how can I think that way? My parents are dead. Terrible way to die.

My hands started to shake uncontrollably; then I burst into tears. The burly cop asked, "Miss Peters, are you OK? Can we get you anything? John," he said to the other cop, "get her a glass of water." After placing the water on the table, he also placed a throw blanket over my knees.

They waited until my neighbor came to keep me company and left me sitting in my favorite chair. She stayed with me, waiting for me to say something yet respecting my silence. Wonderful friend. Eventually, I went upstairs to get ready for bed.

My mother had it right. I would always be running from something.

～～～～～～～～～～

Before I left Plattsburgh for the funeral, my principal found a substitute teacher for my fifth-grade class. I just locked up my two-bedroom house and left. No plants to water, no pets to feed or walk. I am enough. Thank God for Zoloft.

I safely drove the five hours to my hometown, Sleepy Hollow, a little hamlet twenty miles north of New York City on the Hudson River. I pulled into the driveway of my parents' home, larger than most in the Philips Manor neighborhood. A two-story red brick colonial with tall columns, the house proved inadequate for my parents until they added a large, rounded covered porch that offered gorgeous views of the river. I felt my chest tighten every time I came home as an adult. I always wondered if my parents were trying to make a statement of their wealth.

The first time I walked through their house when I returned to town, I actually held onto the walls to keep me upright. All the memories of a scared girl starting a new life seemed to come back at once. My first day at a new school as a senior in high school, hoping no one would know there had been a scandal with my father and his secretary.

Within an hour of my arriving home, Nessa, my best friend since high school, showed up to give me one of her very aggressive, all-encompassing hugs.

Before she could even speak, I said, "I'm not sure how long I'll stay, Nessa. Don't get your hopes up."

Nessa's eyebrows furrowed as she backed away to look at me and then came in for another hug. "Yeah, yeah. I'm just glad you're here, Mija."

Hearing her call me *Mija* made me feel even more at home. It's a term of endearment to Puerto Ricans and Nessa had called me that since high school.

It had been a long time since I lived in town, so Nessa, notorious for never taking time off from her job as a police officer, used three days of personal time to help me navigate writing my parents' obituary for the town newspaper, making the funeral and burial arrangements, planning the luncheon after, and even helping me choose the music to be played. The first thing on our list involved walking across the street from my parents' home to Sleepy Hollow Cemetery to discuss the funeral and burial arrangements. As we entered the driveway and approached the big iron gates, I slowed down and broke into a sweat.

Nessa turned around. "Mija, what's the matter? The office is right up here."

"Yeah, I know. I just need a minute to gather my thoughts."

"You look terrible," she said. "I can't imagine this whole thing is easy. Believe me, I'm not looking forward to it at all when my parents pass."

I nodded. But Nessa didn't know the whole story.

We trudged through the open gates that were bordered by two walkways under stone archways, also gated. Straight ahead were the ivy-covered offices, built with gray and yellow stone. The colors struck me as beautiful, but didn't ease my mind.

During the meeting, I felt distracted thinking about my parents being buried together. There had been a scandal and I could feel a bit of empathy for my mother.

Hmm. Maybe Mother and Father will not be together like I imagined.

"Carrie?" I felt Nessa's hand on my arm, bringing me back to the conversation. "They need a check for the fees."

"Oh, sorry. Sure."

After I wrote the check and we finished with our paperwork, Nessa said, "Let's visit your Aunt Susan's grave. That might help a little to see the place where your parents will be buried before the funeral."

We walked over to the gravesite. My parents would be buried in the Donahue family plot, defined by metal bars outlining the perimeter of the rectangular property. As I looked down on my aunt's grave, I smiled hoping the sisters were reunited. My mother had desperately missed her sister after she died so unexpectedly from breast cancer at forty-seven years old.

Nessa suggested a walk through the grounds. We admired the huge old oak and maple trees, which were just budding and not giving even a hint of their dazzling orange and yellow colors that would come in the fall.

"I don't get the chance to walk through here very often," Nessa said. "Have you heard about some of the historical figures buried here?"

"Well, of course I know about Washington Irving and the Old Dutch Church," I said. "But not too much more."

"Andrew Carnegie, one of the world's wealthiest people, is buried up here on the right. The Astors' graves are behind the mausoleum. I wonder if you know whose grave this is."

I stopped to look at the headstone with the name Elizabeth N. Graham. "How funny," I said. "It only has the date of her death, not her birth."

"Have you heard of Elizabeth Arden, the businesswoman who built an empire with cosmetic sales? This is her grave. She never told people her age. I guess that's the beauty business."

Not paying attention to our path, suddenly we stood in a place I remembered. I blinked in surprise. There stood the Bronze Lady, an imposing statue marking a gravesite. A distant memory swirled in my hazy mind.

"Oh my God," I said. "I feel like I'm going to pass out. Nessa…" I reached for her.

"Carrie, you're so pale! Here, lean against this rock 'til you catch your breath."

After a few minutes of quiet, waiting for the dizziness to stop, Nessa said, "Feel better? This is too much for you. Let's get home so you can rest."

On the way back to the house, I heard someone call my name from behind.

"Carrie! Is that you?"

I turned around, but it took a moment before I recognized him. Still tall and gangly, Chester VanWert had graduated with us and I remembered how he went to the cemetery almost every day in high school, always alone.

"Hi, Nessa," Chester said. "Carrie, so sorry to hear about your parents. Are you home to stay?"

How weird is that? His voice still sounds the same, a high pitch.

Nessa jumped into the conversation. "Carrie's feeling a bit under the weather, Chester. How about if we talk another time?"

"Oh, sure. I'll call you, Nessa. How about next week?"

"OK," Nessa said. "We'll see."

"OK. Don't forget. Bye." Chester stumbled as he backed up.

As she helped me back to her car at my house, Nessa said, "I have coffee at my place." We began the short drive to Nessa's house in Tarrytown.

I hadn't really taken the time to look around when I first drove through the villages. My only goal had been to get to my parents' house. Now, sitting in the passenger seat, I looked at the towns for the first time through new eyes. The villages were composed of Tarrytown to the south and Sleepy Hollow, formerly known as North Tarrytown, to the North.

On the right as we left Philips Manor, we passed the historic site of Philipsburg Manor, a historic museum commemorating a gristmill and trading complex built in 1750.

Driving down tree-lined Route 9 south, I glanced at Sleepy Hollow High School up the hill on the left. The home of the Headless Horsemen, our school mascot. How many other secrets did that school hold besides mine?

As we entered Tarrytown, Patriot's Park came up next on the right with the statue of Major John Andre and the lovely big tulip trees and shallow, slow-moving creek.

"I remember seeing Bobby Kennedy there in the park when he was running for the New York Senate," I told Nessa.

"I was there too!" she said. "But that was before you moved here, right?"

"Yeah. My parents were so excited, especially when Bobby shook my hand. My parents and I felt giddy, as if I were meeting a rock star. Pretty amazing moment in my life."

Nessa nodded. "That was pretty cool for our little town."

Right after the park came Warner Library, built in 1929. Nessa and I spent many hours there, supposedly doing homework, but mostly giggling and flirting with boys.

Struck by the narrowness of Route 9, especially with cars parked on each side, we entered the business district in Tarrytown. As a high schooler though, those narrow streets had helped me feel safe, at least for a while. I let out a deep sigh.

"Almost there," said Nessa. She parked in the driveway of her two-toned green, two-bedroom home.

As the coffee brewed, I felt my body start to relax and feel the warmth of the sun in her kitchen. I had a flashback to sitting in Nessa's mother's kitchen where the family drank strong coffee with a tiny bit of sugar and milk, *cafe con leche*. The coffee always smelled inviting, with aromas of chocolate and caramel. I didn't drink coffee at home; it was never offered. But I enjoyed it on Saturday mornings at Nessa's.

"I can physically see you relaxing, Mija. Your body seems to be melting into the chair."

"Yes, this coffee is amazing," I said. "Do you know

where we could find a bagpiper? My father always loved them."

"I actually think I do. Danny's father belongs to the Knights of Columbus who hired one last year for an event. I'll ask him."

My heart skipped a beat hearing Danny's name. I looked away from Nessa and whispered his name. *Danny, my first and only love.*

~~~~~~~~~~~~~~~~~~~~~~

At the service two days later, about thirty of my parents' new and old friends and colleagues came to honor them. There were many bouquets of colorful flowers on and around the altar and the priest delivered a brief but flattering eulogy. My parents had donated often to the church.

The bagpiper played at the cemetery. The sounds were haunting and I hoped my parents could hear the music in heaven. I couldn't help but remember how my father loved to sing the song, *Danny Boy.*

> *And I shall hear, though soft you tread above me,*
> *And all my grave will warmer, sweeter be,*
> *For you will bend and tell me that you love me,*
> *I shall sleep in peace until you come to me!*

To me, however, I felt conflicted. The music sounded grating. *Wish the bagpiper would finish. I hate this stupid song.*

As the funeral came to an end, I placed two red roses, my mother's favorite, on their coffins before they were lowered. As I leaned on Nessa with our heads together, I whispered that I had become an orphan with no one in the world to love me, except for her.

Nessa gasped. Instinctively, my head jerked to see

what had startled her. There, standing alone in the back of the mourners, stood the person I once loved. I knew him right away although I hadn't seen him in twenty years. Danny. He returned my gaze with a sad smile, and turned to leave the gravesite.

When Ink Bleeds

By: John C. Stipa

Story synopsis:
Struggling author Art Pharos can't catch a break. Rejected by publishers and even his own agent, he heads to Europe in search of inspiration. While touring the home of Jules Verne, he finds an antique quill pen that does more than just write words: it brings stories and characters to life, literally. They live inside The Library Fantastica, a gateway to infinite adventures. The potential of this new-found discovery attracts the attention of forces that put Art in danger. But no one cares for their creations more than an author; and Art's characters won't be erased without a fight. Find out what happens When Ink Bleeds.

Chapter 1

→ Marilyn Alexander snuggled in the deep recesses of a chair in the back of the public library and slid her fingers behind the page of a book. Alert green eyes peered over the top of the cover, spying patrons as they wandered about. She pushed a sheet to the left, her fingers gliding over the crispness of the parchment, her nose breathing in the musty smell of pulp. Never once did she look down at the printed text. The empty chair across from her however, had her constantly wondering if the mysterious young man would brave the cold and take up his usual spot. She pulled her winter parka up around her cheeks and turned another page.

Art Pharos stared at his word processor, re-reading the paragraph he'd typed the day before. His hands hovered above the keyboard, fingers quivering, waiting for his mind to release its creative genius. All of the ingredients were in place: deerskin moccasins, a lambswool sweater, his pipe, and a gentle fire crackling in the fireplace. A glass of port glowed under the kelly green lamp. When Vivaldi burst from the stereo, his fingers attacked.

→Pete Cooper tilted his face away from the fierce January wind and scurried across the parking lot and into the library. A gentle warmth greeted him. He peeled off his scarf and worked his way through the aisles of fiction to his favorite spot. The woman with auburn hair had already burrowed into her chair in the corner. He dropped a hardback novel into the seat and studied her fuzzy boots as she crossed her legs. He held his breath as her hand adjusted the bottom of her sweater that matched the color of her eyes.

Words came fast for Art. Ideas flowed through him, each one fostering more brainstorms. The clacking from the keys fell in step with the music, bouncing from one bookcase to the next. He was in the zone.

→ Looking up, Pete startled to see her staring at him. Her eyes flicked back to the book, a slight crinkle forming at her temples. Pete smiled, hung his coat and leaped his lanky frame into the chair. "Yowch!" He contorted his body, reaching awkwardly underneath him to extract the book. Flustered eyes glanced in the woman's direction. The book in her hands jiggled and he thought he detected muted laughter.

Later that night, after they had conquered their mutual shyness and talked for hours over coffee and cheesecake at a nearby diner, Marilyn carefully penned a bold prediction in her diary: Pete Cooper could be the one.

Two hours later, the fire lay smoldering, the glass of port half empty, and the computer screen filled with content. Smiling, Art interlocked fingers and, leaning back in his chair, cracked his knuckles. Another sip of port helped to savor the moment.

He sent the newborn manuscript to the printer along with a digital copy to his agent, Myrna. She had been representing him for years in pursuit of his first breakthrough novel. Nothing had come to fruition yet, but they kept at it, diligently writing and re-writing in the hope of creating something that would sell.

Rising from the wooden desk, Art punched the off button on the stereo on his way to the printer where he scraped the pages out of the print tray and laid them on the desk. He then drifted to the window, staring mindlessly at the moon.

Art lifted the sash a crack and pressed a wrinkled forehead against the glass. So cool and smooth. He rolled his head from side to side, unable to recall the countless first drafts. Every one rejected by the publisher despite Myrna's best efforts. Too long, too boring, too cheesy. He wondered if this story would suffer the same fate.

His breathing fogged up the window. With a delicate index finger, he traced the letters MA and PC in the condensation. *Don't worry, I'll find a way.* Sighing, Art slugged the remaining port in one gulp. The burn shuddered his body. Kicking off his moccasins, he climbed the stairs for bed.

Author Bios

Claudia Blanchard: I wanted to be either a cultural anthropologist or a poet when I grew up. A retired professor of business, my poems have been published in *Eclipse*, Siena Heights University Press, *Bridges*, Indiana University Press, Cameron Art Museum's *CAM Writers Respond to Art* and Writers of the Forest's anthologies, *It's All Relative(s), Coastal Winds and Other Musings*, and *Longings, Laughter & Laments*.

Terry L. Dismore moved from New York a little over five years ago to a small town in North Carolina. Her home creates a perfect idyllic surrounding with nature and creativity for writing.

Barbara Dullaghan retired from a career in Gifted Education and her nonfiction writing has been published in educational journals as well as by Prufrock Press and Kendall Hunt. She is involved with volunteering for North Brunswick Kiwanis Club and directs a project which provides filled duffle bags for foster children of Brunswick County called "Project Dignity." An excerpt from her novel about Sleepy Hollow, NY is included in this anthology. Barbara grew up there and is very familiar with the magic and energy of the town.

Lorraine Gilmore is originally from Mississippi and has been a resident of Brunswick Forest for five years. In 2001, she retired from an executive placement firm. She began writing essays and poetry in 1974. In 2016, she published Matilde, a picture book for children ages three to eight. In 2017, she organized Writers of the Forest. She is also a member of Seven Bridge Writers Collaborative in Lancaster, MA; she spends the summer months on Cape Cod.

Lee Norman Mehler formerly from New York and New Jersey, retired as an architect in Durham in 2016 and started writing short stories and painting landscapes. He has been published in Forest View and Cape Fear Voices. His piece "The Keys of Life" was awarded Best Original Prose Piece by the Cape Fear Poetry and Prose Society in 2020. Two of his performance pieces, "Alexa… Play Hamilton" and "Strangers in the Garden of Eden" have been filmed through the Port City Playwrights Project. He is honored to have produced the cover art for our three anthologies.

Diane Pascoe is originally from Toronto and has been a North Carolina resident for 17 years. She retired from her career in Human Resources in 2016. When the corporate voices were silenced, she heard her own voice, and thus began her writing career. Her most recent personal humor essay collection, *Honey, Do These Earrings Make Me Look Fat?* was published in May 2021. She has authored two other humor essay collections: *Life Isn't Perfect but My Lipstick Is* and *Never Argue with A Wiener Dog: You'll Lose.* Her essays reflect Erma Bombeck's advice: "If you can't make it better, you can laugh at it."

John Stickney is a poet and writer originally from Cleveland, Ohio and newly arrived to Coastal NC. He has published poetry, non-fiction, fiction and criticism.

John C. Stipa loves the beach, family time, woodworking, playing and coaching sports, traveling, good food and storytelling. He is the author of adventure / mystery / romance novels including *No Greater Sacrifice, The Foiled Knight* and *The Angel Solution*, as well as a Stipa family history: *Johnny No Home, Adventures Growing Up in An Italian Household*. He has also published over ten anthologies with his writing groups.

Suzy Tenenbaum has only poems in this anthology, although she also writes essays and memoir. She was inspired by a poem-a-day challenge for the month of April and caught the poet's bug. Suzy lived 44 years in Vermont, before moving to North Carolina, and loved her role as a consultant and editor for a newspaper column on parenting, in addition to teaching kindergarten. Suzy is now putting focus on writing children's poetry.